PRAYER THAT IGNITES REVIVAL

The Catalyst to Every Spiritual Awakening

JOE ODEN

Chosen
a division of Baker Publishing Group
Minneapolis, Minnesota

Published by Chosen Books
Minneapolis, Minnesota
ChosenBooks.com

Chosen Books is a division of
Baker Publishing Group, Grand Rapids, Michigan

Printed in the United States of America

Library of Congress Cataloging-in-Publication Data
Names: Oden, Joe, author.
Title: Prayer that ignites revival : the catalyst to every spiritual awakening / Joe
    Oden.
Description: Minneapolis, Minnesota : Chosen Books, a division of Baker
    Publishing Group, [2024] | Includes bibliographical references.
Identifiers: LCCN 2023045343 | ISBN 9780800763701 (paper) | ISBN
    9780800772734 (casebound) | ISBN 9781493445066 (ebook)
Subjects: LCSH: Spiritual formation. | Prayer—Christianity. | Evangelistic work. |
    Revivals.
Classification: LCC BV4515.3 .O44 2024 | DDC 248.32—dc23/eng/20231205
LC record available at https://lccn.loc.gov/2023045343

Cover design by LOOK Design Studio

Baker Publishing Group publications use paper produced from sustainable forestry
practices and postconsumer waste whenever possible.

24 25 26 27 28 29 30   7 6 5 4 3 2 1

"A life that was transformed as a result of a prayer and revival movements, Joe Oden is now being used by God to raise the level of prayer maturity in the Body of Christ."

Doug Clay, general superintendent, Assemblies of God

"I have partnered with Joe in revival, prayer, and evangelism. I have witnessed the dynamic anointing on him and the insight the Lord has given him in these areas. He is a gift to the whole Church. If you hope to see the Great Commission fulfilled, read this book!"

Rick DuBose, author, *In Jesus' Name*

"Every generation raises up a voice that can be heard. Joe Oden is being used to build bridges in his generation to call forth a modern-day prayer center for world evangelization. How can he do that? Because he has been anointed by God with a voice that ignites revival unto awakening! Yes, he has!"

Dr. James W. Goll, founder, God Encounters Ministries; author

"Joe Oden has done a great favor for both people interested in revival and those who love prayer. He married the two in such a way that any believer will hunger for more of God."

Cindy Jacobs, Generals International

"I love Joe Oden's new book, *Prayer That Ignites Revival*, because Joe was radically saved and transformed in the Brownsville Revival in Pensacola, Florida. As I read his manuscript, it confirmed so many memories that I cherish of the early years of that powerful move of God. Prayer will always be the prerequisite for Holy Ghost revival. Prayer ignites revival and is the only thing that will sustain it. I am so proud of Joe Oden. God has raised him up as a powerful voice that America and the nations must hear. Don't just go through this book, but allow it to go through you."

John Kilpatrick, founder and executive pastor, Church of His Presence, Daphne, AL

"Our culture stands at a crossroads, and the only answer for this desperate moment is a revival that sweeps our land and radically reorients society. What makes this book especially powerful is that Joe not only writes about awakening, he lives it! His life reflects a passionate, prayer-filled pursuit of revival. Reading these pages will ignite that same passion in you!"

John Lindell, lead pastor, James River Church

"Amid a generation devoid of prophetic plumb lines, Joe Oden fervently calls us back to our knees. Like a road map to awakening, this volume comes as a blueprint to rebuild the altar that has been torn down. May we urgently shed demonic distractions, heed the words of the prophet, and once again cry, 'Send the fire!'"

Levi Lutz, evangelist; director, CFAN Evangelism
Bootcamp, Orlando, FL

"True revival should be heralded by a true revivalist. Joe Oden is one of them. He is a man of intimacy with Jesus, a man of intense love for souls, and a man of incredible intercession. The combination of these is what makes a evangelist one who undeniably carries the heart of God. This book has been written from a pure heart in touch with the heart of the Lord.

It should be the heart of every believer to do whatever it takes in this hour to ignite revival. Joe has given us powerful and proven insights into how to make this happen and to sustain it. You are holding in your hands a valuable resource to challenge and equip you. Be encouraged as you begin the journey, like those mentioned in this book, who ignited revival."

Kim Owens, revivalist; author, *Doorkeepers of Revival,
Just to Make Religion Mad*

"Revivals have never happened by accident or in a vacuum. These historic effusions of glory vary, but have always had one thing in common: that they were birthed in prayer! *Prayer That Ignites Revival* delivers on so many levels, but particularly on the behind-the-scenes ledger of heaven required to tip the scale of an outpouring. I highly recommend Joe Oden's work and believe that this book will change your life."

Sean Smith, cofounder, Sean and Christa Smith Ministries;
author; host, *Keep It 100 with Sean and Christa Smith*

"Joe Oden is a personal friend of mine and, more importantly, a personal friend of God! He is absolutely incredible and preaches what he believes. Fervent prayer is always necessary for us to see personal revival, citywide revival, and global revival. I highly recommend this book to anybody that burns for a deeper walk with Jesus. This will ignite your flame to burn so the world doesn't have to burn for eternity."

Todd White, president and founder, Lifestyle Christianity

To those who have devoted themselves
to pray for revival in the Church
and spiritual awakening in the world.
Jesus has heard your voice and is pouring out His Spirit
upon all flesh in answer to your prayers.

Contents

Contents

Foreword

I have known Joe Oden since he was a new believer, radically saved in connection with the Brownsville Revival. I have known him as a zealous student in our school of ministry, preaching boldly on the streets, unashamed of the gospel. I have known him as a missionaryb whom we sent to Thailand, then as a budding evangelist here in the States, working extensively with the Assemblies of God. And I have watched him become a serious theological student of the Scriptures without losing his fire and passion and burden. Now, as a reader of his book—not as his spiritual elder, former professor, or academic advisor, but as an interested reader—my own heart has been stirred. I believe the same thing will happen to you as you read!

Although I served side by side in the Brownsville Revival with my dear friend and colleague evangelist Steve Hill, laboring day and night together for years and often talking outside of the public meetings, I learned things about Steve's prayer life beyond what I had previously known. It was the same with my esteemed friend and colleague Pastor John Kilpatrick, the man called by God to shepherd the revival. Although I knew his story well and have even interviewed him over the years, I also learned something new. And on and on it goes.

With each new chapter there were new insights, new insights that affirmed and deepened what I always knew: that revival comes in direct response to desperate, persistent, fervent prayer and that the depth of the outpouring corresponds to the depth of the burden. This is what stirred my heart afresh, as I sensed the Lord's call to go deeper in prayer once again and to "seek Him until." Do we really have a choice?

When we cry out, "Revival or we die!", this is not a matter of religious hyperbole or spiritual hype. It is a realistic expression of the urgency of the hour and the critical moment in which we live. Really and truly, without a sweeping move of God in our nation, starting in the Church and then touching the world, America as we know it is doomed. But rather than throw our hands up in despair, we must throw ourselves into prayer—the kind of prayer that Joe describes in this timely, well-researched, and passionately written book.

The best of our human efforts will not work. A superficial gospel will not transform. Our only hope is a holy visitation, and this book can help prepare the way. So read on, and as your own heart is stirred, give yourself to prayer—and don't stop praying until the breakthrough comes. It is time!

Dr. Michael L. Brown, author of *Revival or We Die: A Great Awakening Is Our Only Hope*

Introduction

A Powerful Progression

In 1996 I was court-ordered by a judge to attend church after being charged with drug possession. Up to that point, drugs and alcohol had ruled my life. When a team from the Brownsville Revival came to the church I had picked after being court-ordered, I was radically saved and delivered from drugs. The same night as my salvation, God confirmed my call to be an evangelist. Since that moment, I have lived to preach the Gospel and see those bound by the devil set free, healed, and transformed. As a result of my own transformation, which occurred during the Brownsville Revival, a fire burns deep in my heart for America to experience another Great Awakening, and for other nations to as well.

I have been traveling as an evangelist for well over two decades. In visiting and observing churches across the United States, I find that leaders typically rely on strategy and creative marketing to advance the Church. Many leading voices consider the thought of revival and spiritual awakening archaic and outdated. Countless influential leaders in local churches have largely abandoned key Pentecostal practices, including altar calls, the laying on of hands, the operation of the gifts of the Spirit, and prophetic ministry. In many instances, preaching has shifted away from exhortation, sound teaching, and correction to self-help messages and words of encouragement. I believe this has led to a national decline of the Church in the United States, and in some other countries as well.

Along with the abandonment of these practices is a growing lack of prayer. Church services have become high-paced events with worship and preaching but little to no prayer. This seems to contrast with the early Church's normal operating procedures. Early Church believers prioritized prayer, making it central to their practices. Throughout Church history, many revivals of yesteryear were birthed through prayer. Yet today many churches don't even offer a weekly or monthly prayer meeting, and those that do typically experience low turnout. Leaders who don't prioritize prayer will not see prayer prioritized by other believers around them.

The purpose of this book is to clearly identify the need for revival within the Body of Christ, from a leadership level down to local church attendees. I also will show a clear pathway on how to obtain national, regional, and local renewal, revival, and awakening.

At the start, I want to define a few terms I will use frequently in these pages: *revival, awakening, remnant, prophetic preaching, intercession,* and *renewal.*

Revival: What takes place after something dies or is near death and fresh life is imparted. When an individual, church, or denomination experiences a spiritual decline, apathy, a lack of desire for the things of God, or a coldness toward the moving of the Spirit, renewal of purpose is needed. This revival phenomenon can take place individually, corporately, and even nationally. During this experience, many are saved and set free from a life of sin, the Holy Spirit comes in a fresh way, people encounter God in ways they have never experienced, the operation of the Spirit's gifts is activated on a new level, prayer is elevated, and an entire church or region can be impacted. When someone is near death due to drowning and CPR is administered effectively, the individual is resuscitated and is filled with life once again. This is what takes place in individuals, movements, and nations as God breathes on His people.

Awakening: An occurrence when a nation or region regains an awareness of God after having no desire for the things of God or His Word. This manifestation normally takes place as individuals pray that God will visit a nation or region. It takes place as the Holy Spirit begins to move upon people in a sovereign way. The results are a sudden conviction of sin, a burden over the condition of one's soul, and a heightened level of the manifestations of the Spirit. The outcomes vary, but can include entire cities, regions, and nations being significantly impacted. The impacts can include entire cities coming to Christ, bars closing due to lack of business, police stations with little to no work due to the rapid drop in crime, righteous laws being developed, and full churches throughout a city, region, or nation. This kind of move can come suddenly and without warning.

Remnant: A smaller group of people who possess a different set of beliefs, values, and priorities from the majority of the population in which they reside. They are joined together not by their proximity to one another, but by their shared values and beliefs.

Prophetic preaching: Communication that is not merely intellectual or informational. It can be directed at both those inside and outside the Church, and is the type of sharing that pertains to what God is saying at that moment in history. Prophetic preaching may include some prediction of future events, but more importantly, it is saying what the Holy Spirit is communicating at the present moment.

Intercession: A style of prayer that centers on a felt burden. This kind of communication comes from deep within the praying individual. The results of this form of prayer vary from individual to national breakthrough, and can include awakening, revival, divine healing, the salvation of loved ones, and many other manifestations from God.

Renewal: This takes place in a denomination or network after revival has touched many of the churches that belong in that fellowship or group. It occurs through a fresh outpouring of the Holy Spirit on that group, and it results in the majority of the congregations experiencing an elevated sense of God's presence, a fresh burden for things of the Spirit, and a fresh commitment to the local gathering of believers.

The title of this book is *Prayer That Ignites Revival: The Catalyst to Every Spiritual Awakening*. From the definitions above, you see that revival and awakening are different, and from the title of this book, I trust that you see a powerful progression: prayer, which ignites revival within the Church, which leads to spiritual awakening in the world.

The classic hymn by James M. Gray says, "O Lord, send a revival . . . and let it begin in me!"[1] I pray that this is the cry of your heart or that it is the cry of your heart by the time you finish this book. As you read, I encourage you to give yourself to prayer—prayer that leads to all God has for you, your church, and the world in which you live.

I Want to See Awakening

The Power of Consistency

Steve Hill, whom God used as a catalyst at Brownsville, was a drug addict and drug dealer. He was in and out of jail. Steve gave his life to Christ after years of his mother praying and interceding for him. One time while he was using intravenous drugs, he was tossing up the syringes until several were stuck in the ceiling. His mom looked in and saw what was taking place. She quickly departed, and Steve stumbled to her room, expecting her to intervene and call the police. On the contrary, he found her kneeling, crying out as she prayed for him. She often cried out to God for his salvation.

After yet another bout with the law, Steve was at a low point. His mother's pastor, a Lutheran vicar, came over to the house and ministered to him. That day, Steve repented of his sin and gave his life to Jesus. He was delivered from drugs and began attending a discipleship program called Teen Challenge. After its completion, he attended Bible school under the leadership of David Wilkerson, the devout man of God who had birthed the ministry of Teen Challenge. One of the teachers at the school was Leonard Ravenhill. Ravenhill was one of the most devout men of prayer in the twentieth century and was impacted greatly by the life of Smith Wigglesworth. It has been said that by the end of Ravenhill's life, he would pray eight hours a day. For much of that time, he was contending for revival.

At the early stages of Steve's spiritual formation, he surrounded himself with strong men of God. In his last phone text to me before he passed away, one of the things he said was, "Stay away from the slothful. Flee evil. You have no business hanging around the lukewarm. If you hang around them, you will hang with them!" He encouraged me to guard every relationship. Steve kept his circle tight and didn't associate with those who were not intense and serious about their walk with God, or who told loose jokes, used profane speech, didn't take prayer seriously, and didn't carry a burden for the lost.

This wasn't a form of elitism. Steve carried a sense of purpose and resolve every moment of the day. In his formation, he intentionally sat under men of prayer and holiness, those who believed in the supernatural and had the tenacity to live according to God's Word. This should be practiced today. If you desire awakening and revival, surround yourself with those who have the spiritual discipline and fortitude to see it come to pass. Steve doing just that in his early years would one day produce tremendous fruit.

Revival and awakening don't just manifest out of thin air. It takes a combination of resolute human cooperation and the divine sovereignty of God. When God finds a fully submitted vessel, a praying man or woman, He will be sure to prepare that person for a glorious season of breakthrough. Never underestimate the power of preparation. Never give up in your season when God is molding and preparing you. If you don't give up or give in, you are positioning yourself to be used in an unprecedented way. Remember that God is no respecter of persons (see Romans 2:11). He isn't looking for the one with the highest IQ; He is looking for the Isaiah who is willing to go through the process of preparation: "Then I heard the voice of the Lord saying, 'Whom shall I send? And who will go for us?' And I said, 'Here am I. Send me!'" (Isaiah 6:8 NIV). Are you that person who is willing?

One of the hallmarks of Steve's life was his consistency in devotion and prayer. In Bible school, he would spend a couple of hours a day in secret devotion to the Lord. Note that this wasn't years into his walk with the Lord; it began at the start. Many of those who were close to him in different stages of his ministry would attest that he prayed early and often. There was a drive in him to seek the Lord continually. One thing he would say to me was, "Never stop going after God!" This was his resolve! He was driven to get closer to God and walk in more of His presence throughout his life.

This should be our resolve too—never to be satisfied with where we are, when there are people around us entering into eternity every moment. It is this kind of intensity that keeps us spiritually sharp. Souls are in the balance, and there is no other option. Charles Spurgeon once said, "If sinners be damned, at least let them leap to Hell over our bodies. And if they perish, let them perish with our arms wrapped about their knees. . . . Let not one go unwarned and unprayed for."[1] This embodied Steve's heart and prayer life.

Knowing There Is More

After Steve served a number of years as a youth pastor in West Florida, he and his wife, Jeri, felt God's call to be missionaries. They would go to Argentina to plant churches. During

17

their tenure, eight churches were planted, and a Bible college was started under their leadership. The churches were very strong, one ranging up to five thousand people. Once again, Steve would place himself near those who were serious and steadfast in their prayer life and walk with God. One of those men was Carlos Annacondia from Argentina, known for his powerful deliverance ministry and stadium crusades. They became good friends, so Steve would visit these crusades often. So many people received deliverance at these meetings that they incorporated what were called *demon tents* for those needing freedom. Tens of thousands were saved in these meetings, which included a constant flow of the miraculous. These outdoor meetings would have thousands in attendance every night for thirty to fifty days at a time. Carlos Annacondia is known for making prayer the bedrock for all he does. Steve observed all of this front and center.

One day, one of Carlos's team members asked Jeri if she wanted to see the secret behind the Spirit's great visitation at the meetings. She responded, "Absolutely." They took her to the stage and pulled back a curtain. Under the stage was Maria Annacondia with a group of intercessors crying out to God. This so touched Jeri's heart that this mother of nine and wife of the evangelist would intercede under the stage platform . . . Jeri thought, "I want to be like her." They said this was the secret to what God was doing in the meetings. A deep burden for souls was evident, alongside the proclamation of the Gospel. This combination resulted in the release of God's power in an unprecedented fashion.

Here we observe another layer in Steve's progression. He was now placing himself near a mantle of stadium crusades that demonstrated great power, deliverance, mass salvation, and healing. Steve's faith was being expanded for what God could do through a vessel totally consecrated to the Lord. This is also an example of him keeping his circle tight and only surrounding himself with on-fire, no-compromise leaders. You might be tempted to think you could never get around individuals used in this magnitude. Have you asked God? Have you believed for favor and increase? Try it, and watch what God does. He opens doors no person can shut. I have watched God do this for many, including me.

We must observe as part of Steve's progression that he wasn't coasting or resting on his accomplishments and on the large churches he had planted. He was actively seeking to expand and grow stronger in the Lord. Imagine if he would have become comfortable and would have allowed accomplishment to become his satisfaction—the recognition of being a successful church planter. Yet he didn't settle. In total contrast, he continued to pioneer with a deep knowing that there was something more. Even though he couldn't put his finger exactly on what it was or would look like, he knew there was more.

There wasn't just more for Steve; there is more for you and me. You might say, "I've never planted a church, nor am I even in ministry." At one point, Steve could have said the same thing. Whether you are called to full-time ministry or not, God wants more. "What is more?" you might say. Ask Him. Ask if it's time for you to progress. Smith Wigglesworth was a plumber who got saved and pressed in. He didn't come from a lineage of preachers. Steve didn't come from a line of on fire clergy, but his grandfather was a lay Lutheran minister, and his mother made them attend the Lutheran church religiously. She was a praying mom who never gave up on Steve when he went down a rebellious path of drugs and crime.. He was an ex–drug addict who pressed in and never stopped. Be encouraged and press in to the things of God. Get around people who are on fire. Get around those who move in the miraculous. Get close to men and women of prayer. You will become whom you hang with.

In the latter part of his time in Argentina, Steve began to cry out more intensely, even though he had a strong devotional life. He knew there was more. His wife, Jeri, shared with me a transformative moment. One morning as Steve was praying, she walked into the office and overheard him praying. He cried out in a depth she had never heard before, saying, "Lord, I know how to evangelize, plant churches, do crusades, but God, I don't want to do it in my own strength, I want YOU to do it through me."[2]

Jeri told me something shifted at that very moment—even in her life. She always prayed for Steve, but now it was different. After hearing the depth of his cry to God, she walked out and started weeping in intercessory prayer for Steve, saying, "Yes, God, do it through him, do it through him." That became her cry and lay at the core of her intercession for her husband, knowing that he was the vessel but it was God who would be doing it.

"Always Going after God"

The next crusade Steve would hold after that prayer was in Curicó, Chile. This particular outreach would last around seven days. Note that the entire team would fast for the duration of their ministry time there. In a personal interview with Larry Art on November 1, 2022, he related to me the harrowing details of this trip. The travel from Argentina to Curicó was brutal. The high mountain roads were made of gravel and very muddy. One team member said he was praying in tongues the entire time that they wouldn't slide off the mountain and never be heard from again. The roads got so bad that they didn't think they could make it. A native of the area told them they needed to go through the train tunnel. Talk about the risk to get there! They prayed and set forward. The tunnel was approximately a mile long. Larry told me they were in suspense the entire time that a train could come at any moment and kill them all. However, they got to the other side.

Once the team arrived at the location, they began to set up a stage and sound equipment in a local park. What I'm about to say is not exaggerated: As soon as they began to worship and minister, the Spirit of the Lord descended on the park. The only thing you could compare it to is the Hebrides Revival. The presence of God was so thick that anyone and everyone who drove by the park or walked into it was overwhelmed with the presence of the Lord. Professional businessmen and women would attempt to walk through casually, but they were arrested by the presence of God. One business lady in a suit said, "I cannot move my feet and feel as if they are nailed to the ground."

A Jehovah's Witness approached Larry and said, "What is this I feel? I have never felt anything like this in my life." Car after car began to pull over off the side of the road, with people later expressing that as they were driving by the park, a powerful presence began to fill their car. Larry said the drivers and passengers in the cars began to get saved one by one.

This was a holy invasion. I'm certain God smiled at the dedication of the team. The combination of human cooperation and God's sovereignty was at play. What was taking place couldn't be accomplished through charismatic communication or a well-put-together program. God showed up in power through dedicated, praying servants. Hundreds were saved, vast numbers encountered God in ways they had never experienced, people were delivered of demons, and many were healed.

After the outreach in Curicó, Steve was different. He not only observed those like Carlos Annacondia being used in power, but now God did it through him. His level of faith began to increase, and he felt this was how God wanted to use him from here on out. He believed it was God's will for this kind of power and fruit to happen everywhere. God was fulfilling Steve's cry to work through him. The Spirit of the Lord was now working through him to touch, heal, deliver, and save at a level he had never experienced. Steve felt that God was now transitioning his ministry so he would become more of a missionary evangelist planting churches around the world and holding crusades. He moved to Van, Texas, where he rented a house from David Wilkerson.

Ronnie Roas, Steve's new assistant who moved to Van to serve with him, said that "Steve was always going after God."[3] She attested that until noon or 1:00 p.m. every day, he wouldn't do anything except read the Word and books on revival, and pray. He was consecrated. Ronnie added that he didn't meet with people during the first part of the day. He sought God.

You can see that Steve was continually intensifying his walk with God and didn't get stuck in a rut. He was intentionally deepening his pursuit, seeking to grow. We cannot grow if we don't intensify our devotion and walk with God. Steve went from a couple of hours of devotion a day to four to five hours daily.

Leonard Ravenhill was one of the teachers at David Wilkerson's school, which Steve and Jeri attended. Steve had gotten Leonard's number so he could call and make an appointment with him. Steve wanted Leonard to mentor him. When they arrived, Steve immediately called Leonard, asking to meet. Leonard said, "Yes, I'll see you at 7:00 p.m." Steve responded tomorrow would be better because they'd been traveling all day. Leonard said, "Fine!" and hung up on him. Steve turned to Jeri and said, "He just hung up on me!" So Steve immediately called him back and said, "Seven tonight is fine." When Steve arrived at his door, Leonard handed him a card that read, "Those who are intimate with God will never be intimidated by man." Steve said, "Was this a test?" "Yes," replied Leonard.[4]

Jeri (and Steve himself) told me that Leonard would call sometimes at 4:00 a.m. and say, "What are you doing, Steve?"[5]

Steve would respond, "I'm sleeping, Brother Leonard."

Leonard would say, "I thought you wanted revival!" and hang up on him.

Then on one of those early morning calls, Leonard said something that jarred Steve to the core: "Steve, I have been praying for you the entire night. I have been asking God to use you in a mighty way to bring revival to this nation. You must get serious."[6]

We must note that it was not that Steve wasn't serious. He was a devout man of God who walked in a solid prayer life and lived holy. When your devotional life consists of four to five hours per day, you're serious. Yet at the same time, there is room for everyone and anyone to grow. However, this was yet another progression. It was time for an added level of intensity if he was going to get where God wanted him to be. Steve started waking up at 4:00 a.m. and praying more than normal. The intensity was growing. He wasn't engaged in anything but prayer and devotion until noon every day.

This took place around 1993. Leonard would have eight or ten men come to his house every week and pour into them. David Ravenhill, one of Leonard's sons, said that his dad would share powerful stories with them, such as how he retraced the trail that John Wesley paved as a circuit rider.[7] The only difference was that Leonard and his team didn't have a horse. They were on foot, pulling their supplies in their own strength in a large cart. They would stop in a city or village for a couple of weeks, and during their time there they would pray, do street evangelism, and hold meetings at night. Through this, they planted scores of churches. It was a combination of prayer and evangelism. David told me that one particular night, a man came into a room where Leonard and his team were praying and saw cloven tongues of fire on everyone's head. It was these kinds of stories that continued to fuel the fire for revival deep down in Steve's heart.

As Steve continued to pursue God and hang out with on-fire people like Leonard Ravenhill, the burden for souls came upon him like he had never experienced. It was so intense that he asked Leonard Ravenhill to pray that God would remove it because he couldn't take it anymore. Leonard responded, "I can't do that; I prayed it on you."[8] The intense burden continued to grow.

A few short years after starting to mentor Steve, Leonard Ravenhill passed away, during the fall of 1994. This impacted Steve greatly. He was more determined than ever for God to use him. His heart cry was "Revival or I die!"

Fire Falls on Father's Day

Steve began to visit wherever God was moving. He visited the Toronto Outpouring (also known as the Toronto Blessing) and many other places where the Holy Spirit's activity was evident. On a trip back from overseas, he stopped at Holy Trinity Brompton, an Anglican church in London, England. The vicar was Sandy Miller, whom God was using in a powerful way. Steve went there to receive a fresh touch from the Lord. Sandy prayed for him, and he was hit by the power of God and immobilized.[9] After regaining his composure, Steve got on a plane and returned to America. This was in January 1995.

Something had happened through this laying on of hands. Steve had received an impartation. After he arrived back in America, things began to increase. Steve was traveling throughout the United States, and God was consistently moving through his ministry in an elevated manner he had never yet experienced. Pastors during those early months of 1995 said that when Steve would minister, God would move in ways their church had never experienced in the past.

In Saraland, Alabama, at First Assembly of God, Pastor Ken Draughon accounts that their meetings with Steve were beyond articulation.[10] All the elders were gathered in the green room with Steve just before one service. Steve looked at them and said, "God is going to move." When he said that, they all fell under the power of God.

Pastor Draughon said that the visitation of God during Steve's time there was hard to put into words. He recounted that Steve fasted the entire week:

> He would go out with me, but did not eat anything. The last night, we went to a local Waffle House. As we were walking into the restaurant, a man was standing in the parking lot. When he just looked at Steve, he was hit by the power of God and he fell to the ground, instantly baptized in the Holy Spirit. Then he rolled under one of the cars in the parking lot. It was a powerful manifestation of the Spirit! Steve agreed to return to us the following week, *after* he ministered a Father's Day service in Pensacola, Florida, at Brownsville Assembly of God.[11]

As you may know already, Steve never made it back to Saraland, because on Father's Day 1995 he was scheduled to minister for one service with Brownsville Assembly. Brownsville was in a season where they prayed for revival every Sunday night. Pastor John Kilpatrick was desperate for a move of God. Richard Crisco, the youth pastor at the time, said that Kilpatrick had been preparing the church for revival for six months before the outpouring. All Kilpatrick could talk about on Sunday mornings was how he was hungry for a move of God.[12]

This cannot be glazed over. Steve was spiritually ready and walked into an equally prepared church. The gift of the pastor, who shepherded the people to pursue revival, would now encounter the gift of an evangelist. These two ministry gifts coming together produced great fruit. We must never forget nor fail to appreciate the power of the five ascension gifts and the power that is released when they work together in unison. These are the "fivefold ministry" gifts Jesus gave to the Church after He ascended—apostles, prophets, evangelists, pastors, and teachers (see Ephesians 4:11–12).

Pastor Kilpatrick was in a broken place on Father's Day due to the loss of his mother. He picked up the phone twice to inform one of his leaders that he wouldn't be at the service, but then he felt he had to go. Steve told him God was going to move in power that day. Little did anyone know what would soon follow.

Fire fell on Father's Day like never before at Brownsville Assembly of God. The service lasted until late in the afternoon. When they came back that night, the Spirit of the Lord was so strong that they didn't get out until the sun was coming up the next day. People were mightily saved, and the glory of the Lord filled the room. Pastor Kilpatrick was struck down under the glory of God for hours as God did deep work in his heart.

At 4:00 p.m. that Sunday afternoon, no one had left the church. That's supernatural and doesn't happen unless God is in the room. More than stately buildings, crafted sermons, or gifted musicians, America and other countries need a visitation from God. Yet the nations won't get it unless the Church gets hungry and prays it in.

This Brownsville Revival lasted five years, with nearly 4.5 million people pouring through the doors and close to 250,000 people responding to the altar calls to get right with God.[13] It was not uncommon for services to conclude as the sun was coming up during the first several months. Teenagers were coming to Christ by the thousands, people were receiving calls to go into full-time ministry, miracles were taking place, and holy fire was filling the room every single moment. It was heaven-sent revival.

This wasn't planned or scheduled. You cannot arrange a revival. Revival isn't a set of meetings a church decides to have. A church may call it revival, but that doesn't ensure that it is. People can call a Corvette a pickup truck, but that doesn't insinuate they are right. Revival is a sovereign move of God birthed through prayer and dedication to Him. It is human cooperation with the heart of God, believing in faith for Him to come down. It isn't when a speaker shows up, a favorite worship song is played, or a great teaching is given. It is heaven touching earth in a felt, tangible, holy manner that changes everything. Miracles take place when revival and awakening occur. Individuals who were cold suddenly become engaged and on fire for God. Many receive deliverance from bondages that seemed impossible before the outpouring began. In every sense, revival is hard to explain. It must be experienced.

Revival Starts with a Faithful Servant

I was saved through the ministry of the Brownsville Revival. As I told you, I was bound by drugs and court ordered by law to attend church. A team from Brownsville showed up at the church I had picked to attend. The atmosphere was charged; the preaching was on fire; God was in the room. I ran to the altar as a lost, bound sinner. I got on my knees and cried out to God to take away my reproach, addiction, and filth. He cleansed my soul, forgave my sin, and washed me white as snow. The night of April 27, 1997, after three failed attempts at drug rehabilitation centers, I stood up set free and filled with the joy of the Lord. I was hit by the power that night and immobilized by the Spirit. I arose and never got drunk again, never picked up a joint, never took a line of cocaine. God thrust me out to be an evangelist that very night. I started Bible school a few months later at the Brownsville Revival School of Ministry.

That is revival's fruit. Here are several working definitions of revival, some of which I have taken from Winkie Pratney's book *Revival: Principles to Change the World*:[14]

1. To recall or return from apparent death to life. "Revival brings something back to life that is either now dead or seemingly dead. Revival is not for something that has never lived at all."[15]
2. To return to activity from a state of lethargy. "Revival brings a holy shock to apathy and carelessness."[16]
3. "Recall, return or recovery from a state of *neglect, oblivion, obscurity* or *depression*."[17] Revival calls for individuals to return to truth and obedience that has been erased from memory. The return to truth is often caused by preaching.
4. Revival is when the presence of God permeates an atmosphere. The awareness of God accompanies revival. This phenomenon is no longer by faith, but is a direct manifestation of an awakening of a person, church, city, or nation. Revivals are sustained bouts of time lasting from months to multiplied years. They are not short bursts that last only a few days.

Revival is still in my heart twenty-five years after I was first impacted by it. It's time . . . it's time now for another wave. I believe another Great Awakening is on the horizon. Let's believe and pray it to our shores. *God, send revival! Send revival today!*

Reflecting one last time on the life of Steve Hill, I'm reminded of something God told me a few years back. What one does to get a breakthrough, one must continue to do to keep it and maintain it. Steve fully understood this. He fasted every day of the Brownsville Revival and didn't eat until after the service.[18] The revival went on every night for the first six months. Then at the start of 1996, they revised the schedule slightly and would have a prayer service on Tuesday night and revival services Wednesday through Saturday. This was a deep commitment for Steve. Not only did he fast; he also spent seven to nine hours a day in prayer and devotion. He began his devotion at 8:00 a.m. every day and would conclude at 2:00 p.m. so he could rest before the service. He prayed again from 4:00 to 5:00, and then with the prayer team at 6:00, and then he would spend one to two hours every night praying for people to receive a fresh touch from the Lord.[19] He gave of himself entirely to this move of God.

My desire in this chapter has been for you to see the progression of awakening and revival through the life of a faithful servant. Steve went from glory to glory. He didn't let discouragement rule in the process. He kept moving forward. Here are some keys to the power of consistency that we can see from his example.

- He kept his circle tight, and hung around and was mentored by no-nonsense, on-fire men of God.
- His devotional life was nonnegotiable.
- He was a student of revival and the Word.
- He intentionally sought out people who were used by the Lord. He went out of his way to get close to them and, at the very least, have them pray for him.
- He made great sacrifices to see the power of God through his travels.
- He fasted often.

Remember, this was a twenty-year process in Steve. It didn't happen overnight. Steve progressively matured and intensified his walk, by God's grace. This must be understood. You and I should dream again. If God used Steve to usher in a historical revival, He could use you or me.

Imagine a community area in your city being invaded by the presence of God, just as God invaded in these stories you just read. It bears repeating that this was not an accident. It was divine hunger for souls and a move of God, coupled with the Lord answering in a sobering display that only He can manufacture. We have seen for far too long what humanity can produce; it's time to partner with the Holy Spirit to see what God can do as He works through us when we pray as Steve prayed: *I've worked for you, O God! Now I cry out and ask you to work through me!*

Start Where You Are

God is no respecter of persons; He is looking for someone to be available. Don't let your mind be flooded with excuses as to why you couldn't be the next person God uses to see a city shaken, a neighborhood touched, or an individual rocked by the power of God. When God called Jeremiah, he answered that he couldn't speak and was too young (see Jeremiah 1:6). Jeremiah didn't feel he could articulate well enough, and his vocabulary wasn't as extensive as other people's. Quite possibly, he looked at his own perceived lack of charisma and thought, *No one will listen to me.* He compared himself to others with more experience and qualifications. He might even have thought that he didn't have the finances for such a mission. God reproved and admonished him not to look at what he considered hindrances (see Jeremiah 1:7–8). God encouraged him to put his faith in what He could do through him.

Let this be our focus: *God, work through me. Lord, move through me. Touch me, Jesus, with your power so that I can make a difference.*

May God arrest you this day, and may He put a *"pick me, use me, flow through me"* desire and cry deep down in your spirit.

Where are you in the process? Do you hunger to see an awakening in your generation? Are you hungry for revival? Don't compare yourself and where you are now with where a great general of the faith ended up after decades of pursuit. Start where you are right now. Ask God what He wants you to do, not what He asked Steve to do. It was years in the process for Steve. However, for Evan Roberts of the Welsh Revival in the early 1900s, the process wasn't that long. (We'll look more closely at Evan's life in chapter 9.) God's plan is different for everyone. But one thing remains the same: we must intensify the pursuit if we want an awakening.

God wants to use you. He is inviting you into a process. Are you ready? Draw a circle on the ground and ask God to send revival right there. Set your face toward awakening and don't be deterred or denied. You're in the process, just as others were before you.

You may say, "I'm not called into the ministry." That's the case for many who will read this book. Don't compare yourself to anyone else, however. God will use you where you are. You will play a part in the coming revival. You may say, "I cannot pray seven hours a day, even if I want to." But that may not be God's will for you. Just ask what He wants you to do, and turn up the heat wherever you are. Who knows what God would open if you asked Him to rearrange your life so that you could pray for hours a day. He might just be waiting for you to ask.

There is no such thing as a revival or awakening that doesn't have a genesis. Pastor John Kilpatrick of the Brownsville Revival said, "Never forget: Revival does not start with a denomination, a church, or a city. It always starts with an individual."[20] The embryonic conception often starts years or decades before an awakening or revival occurs. May the conception of awakening start with you right now.

IGNITING PRAYER

Jesus, I ask you today to speak to my heart and change my life. Tell me in what ways you desire me to intensify my devotion. Give me an unquenchable hunger for awakening and revival. Let my desire for a nation-shifting move of God never cease, no matter how long it takes or what sacrifices you ask of me. Let this be the intensification of my cry for revival, the embryonic conception of my cry that will never die. Send the fire today! Jesus, I ask you to set me ablaze with your holy fire! In your name, Amen!

I Will Not Be Denied a Breakthrough

The Power of Determination and Fortitude

When we observe the world and the United States of America, it doesn't take long to arrive at the conclusion that the nations are in desperate need of a heaven-sent awakening. If charismatic preaching and well-to-do events were going to cause mass repentance and open heavens, it would have occurred a long time ago. America and countries around the globe don't need a new strategy, nor someone with a high IQ or PhD. The need is far more robust. It is awakening or bust, revival or we die.

You may say, "Joe, God is moving at my church." That's fantastic! But it is far from a national awakening or revival. Awakening impacts culture and brings entire nations back to God. Sin and depravity lead people and nations far from God, which leads to sin-filled societies where everyone does what is right in their own eyes.

The question could be raised, "How do we know that we're in need of an awakening?" Can I be vulnerable for a moment and share a story that shows an indicator that my home country, America, which is a microcosm of the modern world, is in desperate need of a God-sent awakening? My wife and I have three children. A couple of years back, my seven-year-old daughter received an assignment in school that was sent home due to a massive ice storm that hit our city. The school was closed, but assignments were given for the week so students wouldn't fall behind and get off schedule.

Every assignment seemed normal, but one caused my wife and me to be particularly alarmed. Trisha, my beautiful wife, is a very good mother. She was looking over the assignments so our daughter could complete the work. One task said our daughter needed to watch/listen to a song and then write down her emotions after viewing it. The teacher attached a YouTube video link, so Trisha wanted to see the content first. After viewing it, she called me in panic to take a look. I could tell she was very disturbed. As I watched it, I was shocked at the content. It was beyond sexual and included drag queens/cross-dressers dancing and prancing around as they served a boy band about to sing.

Remember, my daughter is only seven years of age. Her assignment was to write down her emotions. She wasn't even old enough to understand heterosexuality, let alone homosexuality. To be clear, I was not okay with this, nor would I have been if it had contained sexually explicit material between heterosexuals. To make a long story short, the principal and teacher deeply apologized as we confronted the school over this egregious infringement on my seven-year-old's innocence and purity. Apparently, if this assignment had been given in class, students would have closed their eyes and only listened to the lyrics. The school assured us it would never happen again.

However, the fact that it happened in the first place reveals that this country desperately needs a spiritual awakening. The reality that there's debate over drag queens being part of small children's education reveals that America is living in a time of utter decadence. I would also feel the same outrage if it were straight people acting sexually suggestive. There are schools that allow people dressed in full drag apparel to come into the classroom and read to our kids. This is bad by itself, yet we are also debating sex-change medications for children under the age of twelve. This is unfathomable and evil. It's outrageous, and these children haven't even reached the age of puberty, much less developed the cognitive ability to make a decision of this magnitude.

A number of states allow kids under eighteen to have abortions without a parent's permission, and some states are also looking to legalize giving children puberty-blocking treatments and hormonal therapy without parental consent. This is heartbreaking! Stately church buildings and leaders' charisma won't change this. We need an awakening.

We also have states offering to subsidize women coming in to have an abortion if they live in a state where abortion is not permitted. The reality is that a large segment of the populace doesn't see abortion as murder and a sin against God. The safest place in the world should be in a mother's womb.

The number of people who are living together outside wedlock and the rise of children coming into the world without both parents in the home are such travesties. Fornication is normative in society. Alcoholism and casual drug use are no longer on the fringe. The fear of God has been lost. The only hope is for God to have mercy and send a spiritual awakening.

In a personal interview with author and physician Dr. Paul Saba, he told me this:

Quebec, Canada, has the highest percentage of euthanasia and assisted deaths in the Western World since this practice was legalized in 2016. At the beginning of the Canadian law, only those who were terminally ill had access. Now, many people with nonterminal conditions are being euthanized, including those with chronic conditions but lacking social supports such as affordable housing. They can get euthanized because "their lives have become unbearable" for a myriad of economic and social reasons. In March of 2024, euthanasia will be legalized for people with mental health challenges (depression, anxiety, eating disorders, autism, Asperger's, personality disorders, schizophrenia). This will happen despite the fact that psychiatrists cannot definitely predict who will get better with appropriate treatment. Ongoing discussion is now taking place to euthanize children. Some children who are considered "mature minors" may be euthanized by physicians without parental consent.[1]

Yes, children would be able to commit suicide through the hands of a doctor, and the parents wouldn't be notified to make funeral arrangements until the deed was done. This is none other than the work of Satan in full effect. It's not even hidden anymore.

"Right in My Eyes"

This is not the first time nations have needed God to have mercy. The Western world of today and Israel during the time of the Judges have some striking similarities. There are few books throughout the Bible that show the lows of human depravity the way Judges does.[2] The Israelites pledged to obey God prior to Joshua, yet departed from their oath and bowed to idols, intermarried with pagans, and accepted the foreign gods of their wives. Morality was all but gone as a son stole from his mother and an entire tribe permitted and tolerated homosexual rape, along with rape-murder (see Judges 19:22–30).

Tragically, there were times when bouts of civil war occurred. Ephraim was devastated by Manasseh, and the tribe of Benjamin was nearly completely wiped out by its own countrymen (see Judges 12; 20–21). Between the times of Joshua and Samuel, Israel fell to a tragic low of spiritual and moral disaster. Repeatedly, judgment followed sin and rebellion, and blessing followed prayer and repentance, albeit repentance is only mentioned in one section of Judges (see Judges 10:10, 15). The people prayed much more than they repented and turned from their sin. At times, God raised up individuals like Deborah and Gideon, whom He used to turn Israel back to Himself. However, these intervals of revival were sparse and very brief.

By the time of Samson, who served as a savior judge in Israel, the nation began to plunge into greater depths of depravity. Calling Samson immoral would be understating his depraved condition. He was set apart from birth to be a Nazarite, which meant a commitment not to drink anything fermented, cut his hair, or marry a foreign woman. He didn't adhere to the standards of his call. His flesh led him, not the attributes of someone committed to the Lord. Samson made a statement that would become a theme for Israel as it spiraled into gross idolatry and immorality. He stated in a decision to marry a foreigner, "Get her for me, for she is right in my eyes" (Judges 14:3).

This statement was a glimpse into his heart, and in all reality, into the heart of the entire nation. Samson wasn't following God's decrees, but his own fleshly desires. Even in this sinful state, he prayed at times, as recorded in Judges 15:18 (NIV): "Because he was very thirsty, he cried out to the LORD, 'You have given your servant this great victory. Must I now die of thirst and fall into the hands of the uncircumcised?'" Even though he prayed, it did not put him in right relationship with God. After divorcing the Philistine woman, he then had an affair, or at the very least a onetime sexual encounter, with a prostitute (see Judges 16:1). With both the Philistine girl from Timnah and this prostitute, he looked on them with his eyes and was led by sensual desires: "Samson went down to Timnah, and at Timnah he saw one of the daughters of the Philistines" (Judges 14:1). Samson sees, he wants, he takes.[3] Once again, he embodies his previous statement, doing what is "right in my eyes."

Samson submitted to nothing but his flesh. He lived by his own standards and not God's. His governing appetites led him, not God.[4] There was seemingly no reflection or contemplation about God's call or will for his life. As professor and commentary author Daniel Block points out,[5] here are just a few of the many violations Samson undertook:

- Intermarriage with non-Israelites was forbidden by the Lord, yet Samson did not adhere to this statute (see Deuteronomy 7:1–5).
- In Exodus 20:14, God commanded, "You shall not commit adultery." Yet there is no indication that Samson ever considered this a violation or was ever convicted of this sin. His standard was *if Samson wants it, he gets it.*
- As leader of Israel, Samson was not above reproach or self-controlled, among other character flaws. Yet Scripture says, "Therefore an overseer must be above reproach, the husband of one wife, sober-minded, self-controlled, respectable, hospitable, able to teach, not a drunkard, not violent but gentle, not quarrelsome, not a lover of money" (1 Timothy 3:2–3).

Being led by his sensual desires eventually culminated in Samson's downfall. He fell in love with yet another Philistine.

Scholars believe that due to her proximity and the way she behaved, Delilah was most likely a Philistine.[6] The fact that she would turn him over to the Philistines supports this claim. A major reason God didn't want Samson or other Israelites to marry foreign women was that He knew they would be tempted to take on these pagan wives' gods. This happened time and time again throughout Israel's history. When Israelites married foreign women, they turned from the Lord and fell into idolatry.

The back-to-back sexual affairs show striking continuity. Samson didn't hide sleeping with a prostitute, nor his sexual affair with Delilah. These were done openly, without any discretion. Judges 16 (NIV) shows that the people in the city watched him come and go: "The people of Gaza were told, 'Samson is here!' So they surrounded the place and lay in wait for him all night at the city gate. They made no move during the night, saying, 'At dawn we'll kill him'. . . . The rulers of the Philistines went to her [Delilah] and said, 'See if you can lure him into showing you the secret of his great strength and how we can overpower him so we may tie him up and subdue him'" (vv. 2–5). There is nothing in Scripture revealing any feelings of shame in Samson or suggesting he tried to hide his immorality. Despite his supernatural strength from God, we find no mention of conviction. Instead, evidence shows he had lost any conviction over sin . . . if he even possessed it in the first place. His immorality was wide open to the public. His leadership and example were tepid. Instead of leading young men in holiness and godliness, he was leading them in the exact opposite direction.

Samson's sexual sin would be his demise. Delilah would betray him by coaxing him into telling her how he could lose his great strength. After she cut his hair, which was the key, the Philistines moved in and gouged his eyes out, beat him, shackled him, and took him as a political prisoner (see Judges 16:15–21). His hair would later begin to grow back, and he would kill a multitude of Philistines by collapsing the building where many of them gathered. In this process, he pushed the pillars that held the structure up, and he died with them (see vv. 22–31). What a tragic ending. It didn't have to end like this. Even though he took out more of the enemy in his last feat, he could have gone out with a much better testimony.

Samson's blatant turning up his nose at God's edict wouldn't bring Israel to any type of repentance. We must note that just because Samson had some sort of prayer life didn't mean he was right with God. The fact that God used him didn't validate his actions or indicate God's approval. Many today state they are not convicted while living with someone outside marriage. They attend church, lift their hands during worship, and confess they feel the presence of God. There's no doubt that they probably do feel it, just as Samson did when the Spirit of the Lord would rush upon him (see Judges 15:14). I've also watched young Christian men and women alike seek relationships with people outside the Christian faith. I have yet to see it end well. Most often, the believer is tempted into sin and immorality. The New Testament states explicitly, "Do not be unequally yoked with unbelievers. For what partnership has righteousness with lawlessness? Or what fellowship has light with darkness?" (2 Corinthians 6:14). Feeling a lack of conviction is not an argument. The heart is deceitfully wicked. Bluntly, I would submit that to follow one's own desire is the overarching sin of Samson and the people of the book of Judges. They did what was right in their own eyes and not in the eyes of the Lord. The same happens today. God's Word trumps inner feelings and personal convictions, not the other way around.

Depravity's Downward Spiral

The downward spiral of sin continues in Israel until the very end of Judges. Judges 17 shares the narrative of a man named Micah, who steals 1,100 pieces of silver from his mother. When he hears his mother utter a curse on the one who stole it, he gives it back to her. What she says afterward is either the epitome of complete ignorance about the Lord's statutes or blatant rebellion. Both scenarios are bad. The mother consecrates the silver to the Lord. This seems very noble and sacrificial. In the same breath, however, she encourages her son to idol worship by making a carved image with two hundred pieces of the silver. This is the height of antithesis and unequivocally contrasts God's Word. It makes absolutely no logical sense, yet Micah agrees. He places the image in his personal shrine and throws in some additional idols. Then he hires one of his sons as a priest (see Judges 17:1–6). A priest outside the Levitical order cut against the very fabric of the regulations God had set for priests.

The fact that this man's name was Micah connotes that they understood what they were doing. Micah means, "Who is like Yahweh?"[7] This is a rhetorical question, and the answer is simple: "No one!"[8] The fact that this mother committed her son to Yahweh and not Baal underscores that she in all respects was in covenant with God. Yet this woman was completely deceived. She might have believed she was in covenant, but her actions were far from depicting a covenant relationship.

This depiction of the acts of Micah and his mother typified all Israel. Everyone did what was right in their own eyes. This is in direct contrast to the Scripture "And you shall do what is right and good in the sight of the LORD, that it may go well with you" (Deuteronomy 6:18).[9]

Micah possibly felt his cult wasn't fully legitimate because he didn't have a Levite as priest. He solved that problem when he stumbled upon a traveling Levite and offered him a job to be the father and priest of his idols and shrine. The young Levite, who should have known better, took the position. The money was good and the accommodations were generous, so he sold out (see Judges 17:7–13).[10]

After hearing Micah's offer to become his personal priest, this Levite should have denounced his offer and warned him that God forbade idol worship (see Deuteronomy 13:6–11). Instead, he takes advantage of this opportunity and capitalizes on it. Because of the prestige and notoriety that came with the position, along with the money, he doesn't warn Micah. In contrast, he joins in and gives support to these cultic practices, showing partiality due to this man's money.[11] As commentary author Daniel Block tells us,

> In the words of Malachi, the heirs of "the covenant of Levi" have corrupted their high calling. Instead of serving as an agent of life and peace, revering Yahweh and standing in awe of his name, offering truthful and righteous instruction, walking with Yahweh in peace and uprightness, turning Micah back from iniquity, preserving knowledge, and serving as a messenger of Yahweh of hosts, this Levite has himself self-apostatized.[12]

Israel's downward spiral didn't stop there. Angry mobs soon demanded homosexual relationships by any means necessary, including rape, and gangs would also rape innocent women and leave them for dead (see Judges 19:22–28). Civil war ensued, where clans would murder other clans (see Judges 20). Men would kidnap and steal wives for themselves without the women's consent (see Judges 21). Utter moral chaos was the theme. Israel had backslidden and was in breach of its covenant with God. This was one of the lowest points in Israel's history.

This story has similarities with that of the modern West in the twenty-first century. As those in ancient Israel did what was right in their own eyes, so is the tone of the large majority of the West. Israel would pray, but didn't practice repentance. Make no mistake about it—there will never be revival or awakening without authentic repentance and a turning away from sin. Let me state that this is not a political issue, yet when politicians use the Bible to justify abortion, their apostasy deceives many. When members of the clergy submit that Jesus was okay with homosexuality, this is indeed a cocktail from Satan. When leaders invoke the idea that Jesus gives everyone the right to choose their sexual orientation or that people are born homosexual as a biblical foundation, society has become depraved. The West is no longer on its way to depravity and decadence; it has arrived.

These times are not calling for more prosperous (well-to-do) events or dynamic, charismatic speakers; they call for a great global awakening. The call is for *every* believer to stand with fortitude and with determination that we will not bow to this kind of apostasy and debased radicalization. God is looking for those like Jeremiah, to speak the truth amidst corruption and not bow to cultic practices, as did the Levite in Judges 17. The time calls for a determination that beacons from deep down inside, no matter what the cost.

You may say, "What can I do? I'm but a youth." Jeremiah said the same thing (see Jeremiah 1:4–19), but God used him as one of the strongest prophetic voices and proponents of national revival the world has ever known. Or you may ask, "How can God use me? I'm too old." Remember, God raised up Abraham at the age of ninety-nine and Sara at ninety (see Genesis 17:1–17). You may say, "My educational status leaves me unqualified." Never forget that it was said of Peter and John that they were unschooled, ordinary men (see Acts 4:13), yet God used them to turn the world upside down. Or you may give the excuse, "I'm far from perfect." Thankfully, perfection is not a prerequisite for being used by God.

The atmosphere of sexual sin and depravity didn't even escape the house of the Lord during the period of the judges. Eli, who served as a priest at Shiloh, had two sons who served with him in God's house (see 1 Samuel 1:3). One was named Hophni, and the other Phinehas. The Bible calls them wicked and says that "they had no regard for the Lord" (1 Samuel 2:12 NIV). They scoffed at His Word. Having "no regard" shows that they didn't know, acknowledge, or recognize Him.[13]

Instead of caring for the people, Eli's sons showed them contempt by thrusting a fork into the pot or kettle and taking uncooked meat for themselves whenever anyone offered a sacrifice.[14] The fat had yet to be burned off, which was supposed to be done first in honor of Yahweh (see Leviticus 3). These men were gluttons. The priests were already allotted the breast and right leg (see Leviticus 7:28–36). The contempt for Yahweh's offering was egregious and was an outright liturgical offense (see 1 Samuel 2:13–17). If the worshiper reminded Hophni and Phinehas of their infraction, these thugs would threaten to take the meat by force.

Stealing from God's people and showing contempt for the Lord's offering is bad enough, yet these men were immoral also. Their sexual escapades were ongoing, and Eli heard about them numerous times.[15] They were having sex with the women who served at the entrance to the tent of meeting (see 1 Samuel 2:22). This was outright abuse of these women, even if it was consensual. Instead of instructing them in their service to the Lord, Hophni and Phinehas were pouring out their lust upon them and using their priestly office to fulfill their carnal desires.

Eli rebuked his sons for their wickedness, but there's no mention of discipline or discontinuing their employment. He allowed them to continue in their role, and they continued in their immorality (see 1 Samuel 2:22–25). Their behavior was exactly opposite of God's standards for a priest. Yet Eli's sons didn't care what God's Word said; they simply followed the book of Judges' theme of doing what was right in their own eyes and living to please the flesh. In continuity with Samson, they took what they wanted.

When we consider the need for national awakening during the time of the judges, the task couldn't seem more daunting. Political leaders didn't have the people's interests at heart and were outright hostile to the things of God. Priests in the service of the Lord winked at sin or were full partakers in rebellion against Him. The people followed suit in idolatry and chaos. How could this ever shift? Was God through with Israel?

Absolutely not! He needed someone with resolve, fortitude, and determination. *Note that God doesn't need an army; He only needs a remnant.* It doesn't have to be large; it just needs to be a few determined individuals, and they can move heaven and shake earth.

A Righteous Remnant

This was the very place that God found a righteous remnant. Elkanah, Hannah, and Samuel are presented in stark contrast to Eli, his sons, and the other notorious characters in the book of Judges.[16] Elkanah would prove himself a mild-mannered, kind, and loving husband. This was quite the opposite of the men described in Judges 19–21.[17] Hannah would prove herself a devout woman of prayer. The truth should not be overlooked that this was a devout, God-fearing family unit. They weren't like the characters in the latter half of Judges, and the character of the person praying is just as important to God as the prayer: "The prayer of a righteous person is powerful and effective" (James 5:16 NIV).

A great number of God followers aren't depicted here; just one family, to be exact. Certainly there were more, but it isn't in the narrative at the end of Judges, nor at the beginning of First Samuel. In this story, a devout family walks into the house of God. It was their tradition to go yearly to God's house, where Eli and his two wicked sons presided (see 1 Samuel 1:3). This trip seems to be a private time of extra devotion for Elkanah and his family, not one of the three required trips for all males to make to present themselves before Yahweh every year.

Once again, look at this family's sincere devotion. Whenever they would go to the house of the Lord, they would sacrifice to Him. In the process, Elkanah would give portions of meat to Peninnah, who had children, but he would give a double portion to Hannah, who didn't have any children because the Lord had closed her womb (see 1 Samuel 1:3–5). Society viewed the closing of her womb as the judgment of God upon her life, yet there was no indication of this being judgment in the text.[18] However, society, and especially Peninnah, wouldn't be so kind.

Imagine if everywhere you went, there was an undertone of gossip that you were being judged by God. Hannah's value as a woman was under duress. At that time, a woman's glory was her ability to produce children. Hannah was unable. The resulting combination of ridicule and slander caused her unbearable anguish.

Peninnah's specific provocation of Hannah was unending and relentless (see 1 Samuel 1:6–7). Imagine the stigma you'd carry if society believed you had grieved God to the point of judgment. Think of the countless accusations made against Hannah: *She must be an idolator! Maybe she's an adulterer or a thief!* None were true. She was a devout, righteous woman of God.

Yet this situation would distract Hannah from the goodness and promise of God. There is no mention of her praying at this point. She is only focusing on what God is seemingly not doing, instead of what He can do. Anytime we focus on what God is not doing, a belief system can be built of doubt and unbelief. We aren't called to focus on what God has not done, but only on what He has said He would do and has done. Our focus in dire circumstances should be on thoughts like these:

> "No weapon forged against you will prevail, and you will refute every tongue that accuses you. This is the heritage of the servants of the LORD, and this is their vindication from me," declares the LORD (Isaiah 54:17 NIV).

> If God is for us, who can be against us? (Romans 8:31 NIV).

> But he was pierced for our transgressions, he was crushed for our iniquities; the punishment that brought us peace was on him, and by his wounds we are healed (Isaiah 53:5 NIV).

Even though Hannah wasn't focused on what God could do, her focus was about to shift. The devil's objective is to keep the righteous focused on the problem, the pain, the turmoil, and the depression. He will use anyone and everyone to do so. He used those in the crowd that led the way to try to thwart Bartimaeus (see Luke 18:35–39). The dissenters of Nehemiah constantly tried to get his attention focused on the state they were in instead of the miracle God was about to perform. If the enemy can use your dad, brother, wife, son, boss, or even pastor to shift your focus to doubt and unbelief, he will. Don't fall for it. Pick your head up in fortitude and determination, and set your face toward God.

Hannah was on the brink of doing just this. In the midst of all the circumstances we looked at—the depravity in and out of God's house; a nation that had turned its back on God;

idolatrous cults that had formed—in walks an intercessor. In walks a woman who would cry out to God. In walks a woman who would rend the heavens and shake the earth through her personal devotion and prayer. In walks a woman who would garner the very attention of God Almighty.

Hannah turns her face to the Lord in anguish and bitter weeping, and she specifically prays for God to open her womb and give her a son (see 1 Samuel 1:10–11). Note that Scripture doesn't say she came in joy and happiness. Just because she was depressed and in pain didn't mean she couldn't begin to seek the Lord. It isn't about an emotion, feeling, or sense. It is about a person's determination and made-up mind to turn his or her face to the Lord.

This was a determining factor in Hannah's life. She now possessed a mind that was made up. There is power when one's mind is made up and set on the things of the Lord in dire circumstances. From Daniel during the days of Babylon, to Noah in a day of great wickedness, to the times of the oppression through Pharaoh, God always has a praying remnant who have not given in or bowed their knee to the spirit of the age. God has a segment who are always galvanized with fortitude and determination. Hannah was such a one.

Called to Be Such a One

God is calling you right now to be such a one. Will you? Will you pick up the mantle of a past intercessor in the midst of a depraved world and believe God for a Great Awakening? If not you, then who? If not now, then when? It's time to pick up the mantle and believe!

You may say, "I have begun." Don't stop! Let's observe what happens to a nation when an intercessor refuses to give in and has his or her mind made up. In contrast to the norm of her culture, Hannah makes a vow to God and commits to give her son to the Lord all the days of his life (see 1 Samuel 1:11). At the time, God was indeed in need of someone to speak for Him since "In those days the word of the LORD was rare; there were not many visions" (1 Samuel 3:1 NIV). Just as Hannah was barren of children, the earth was void of prophetic unction or God's word, from leadership or anyone else, for that matter. The people were doing what was right in their own eyes, but here Hannah is, doing what is right in the eyes of the Lord. She commits her son to be a Nazarite, holy and set apart to the Lord.

Observe the powerful contrast in regard to the way Hannah prays and the prayers of others in the context of Judges.[19] She prayed *before* the Lord, in the presence of God, which depicts that He was near her: "As she continued praying before the LORD, Eli observed her mouth" (1 Samuel 1:12). Others in Judges were described as praying "to the Lord." Hannah's prayer shows there was less distance between God and her because she prayed *before* Him and not *to* Him. The manner of her prayer emphasizes the presence of Yahweh, whereas other people's prayers emphasized a direction, implying more distance from Him. While it's not solely about the prayer, the prayer has much to do with the effects of praying.

Also note that Hannah kept praying before the Lord. She didn't stop. There is power in a made-up mind determined to get a breakthrough. The Word of God is full of examples of this, from Daniel, to Esther, to the apostles, and many more who didn't stop in the face of resistance or persecution until God moved on their behalf. The times we find ourselves in now call for this kind of praying. We must never give in, never give up, never quit. The day and hour in which we live call for determination and fortitude like never before.

Hannah's fortitude and determination would be put to the test. In the midst of her desperate, broken, and heartfelt prayer she gets rebuked. Eli accuses her of being a drunk. It had been so long since God had moved here that Eli couldn't discern heartfelt prayer in the presence of God from a drunken stupor. What a low point for the people of God. This was an orchestrated tactic of the devil. Using Eli, he was trying to offend Hannah right in the middle of a prayer that was on the verge of a breakthrough. This is a never-ending ploy of the enemy against the people of God. When a breakthrough is at hand, he will attempt to steal it at the last second. His attacks are always the most fierce at the finish line.

In Luke 5, it's explicit that the Holy Spirit desired to heal everyone: "And the power of the Lord was present to heal them" (Luke 5:17 NKJV). However, only one person was healed—the paralytic let down through the roof. Why? Because many in the room were offended at how Jesus had healed him and what He had said during the healing. There is zero ambiguity in Luke's words: "to heal them" is plural, not singular. When an offense is present, however, it shuts down the flow of the miraculous—even through the ministry of Jesus.

In Mark 11:20–26, Jesus exhorts us that if we have faith in God, we can move mountains. The mountain simply means the impossible. Yet if you have faith to move a mountain and also have offense, that offense will shut down the effects of your prayer and snuff out the power of faith—no matter how much you pray. Offense is a top-utilized strategy from hell itself to keep people bound, sick, depressed, and in many other bondages. However, overcoming offense and praying the prayer of faith is a powerful combination that is a threat to hell itself.

How would Hannah respond to Eli? She responds in humility and brokenness. She also speaks respectfully to Eli, who was placed in his position by God. This is also an attribute we must maintain—respect for authority. Hannah could have said, "Your sons steal from God's people and are sexual perverts, and you allow it." But she didn't respond like that. You can be right and wrong at the same time. She could have been right, and then left offended and still barren. Her humble and honoring response to Eli's false claim about her produced a miracle (see 1 Samuel 1:14–19).

Even though the word of the Lord was rare in that time, Hannah's broken and contrite prayer, coupled with humility, fortitude, and determination, produced a miracle. Eli prophetically spoke to her and said to go in peace and that God would grant her the petition. God answered her prayer, and she conceived (see 1 Samuel 1:20–28). Through her determination and fortitude, her prayer produced life out of a barren place. This process of prayer isn't complex, nor is it easy. It doesn't take depths of education, but neither does a breakthrough come without a fight. Eloquence and sophistication aren't a prerequisite, though the miracle oftentimes doesn't come without a fight.

You may ask, "How do I get a breakthrough? How will God use me to birth awakening and revival in my school, workplace, or neighborhood?" The answer isn't deep, yet it takes more than most are willing to pay. You must pray through the pain, and persist in the midst of the depravity and moral decay around you. Again, never stop, never give in, and never quit. Stay before God and simply request that He pour out His Spirit in your context, until He does. Just like Hannah, you, too, will see a miracle.

Hannah's miracle didn't stop at the birth of Samuel. No! Remember that Samuel was used to bring spiritual renewal to all Israel. His mother's prayer birthed a prophetic movement that shook a nation and brought it back to the Lord. Samuel anointed David, who cut down Goliath. Have you ever thought of Hannah when you read the story of David and Goliath? Yet there wouldn't have been a national victory if there hadn't been a hidden intercessor. David goes on to bring Israel into her greatest height under his kingship and that of his son. Without Hannah, this would have only been a dream.

Isaiah prophesied that from the line of Jesse, David's father, would come Jesus the Messiah (see Isaiah 11). God used Hannah in the midst of her pain and depression to open the way for Jesus to come. Never, I mean *never*, underestimate the power of determination and fortitude behind prayer. If Hannah would have caved, the story would be different. But she didn't. She pressed in until breakthrough. She tarried until awakening was birthed and a national breakthrough ensued.

Hannah is gone, but her prayer life lives on and is still felt today. Your prayer life can be felt for generations to come as well. You can see national breakthroughs too! If God used Hannah, He could use you. Now, set your faith toward heaven and don't stop praying and seeking until God breaks in and breaks out. The time is now! You are God's choice! Go for it!

IGNITING PRAYER

God, I ask you to forgive me of any sin, known or unknown. I understand that every heaven-sent revival and awakening must include repentance.

Jesus, I plead with you to awaken my nation. You see the depravity, sin, and rebellion. Our only hope is you.

Holy Spirit, I ask you to use me as you did Hannah, to pray until something breaks and revival is birthed. Give me the resolve and fortitude she possessed never to quit, back down, or give up. Help me persevere with faith, even when I don't see what I want to see on to my timetable, and help me inspire others to join me.

I commit to you, Jesus, that I will press in until I see revival with my own eyes. In your name, Amen.

I Will Confess the Sins of My Nation

The Power of Repentance

American evangelist Frank Bartleman was reported to say, "The depth of our repentance will determine the depth of our revival."[1] The same can be said of nations. Nations that fall into gross idolatry and sin will experience national revival and awakening that is determined by their depth of turning and repentance. Deep repentance is needed when countries like many in the West embrace and legalize sin on a national level (such as the sin of abortion; certain states in my country are protecting doctors instead of the unborn). The time for prophetic preaching is upon the West like never before. This hour calls for the gift of the prophet to rise and shine. The word of the Lord is not "peace, peace" amid such egregious rebellion against the statutes of God. Like never before, the time calls for a spirit of John the Baptist and Jeremiah.

The old adage is true that there is nothing new under the sun. Many times throughout history show that Israel turned from God to gross idolatry and suffered the ensuing judgment. Yet other times also show that with repentance and the turning of hearts, God releases spiritual awakening and renewal. The Word of God shows that there is hope for nations who heed the prophetic word of godly prophets. Sadly, it also shows judgment when they do not.

God judged Israel for its state of rebellion after the people refused to listen to the prophets. In this hour, the current state of the West calls for mass repentance, or there will be anything but an awakening. Arguments could be made that we are living in a moment when it will be awakening or judgment—revival or bust.

In this chapter, my goal is to show hope and a future amid depravity. First, however, we must look at an example of when repentance went unheeded. When citizens and rulers fail to confess their sins and the sins of their nation, the outcome is bleak. Israel was in the midst of a moral collapse during the days of Jeremiah the prophet. The nation found itself overthrown by Babylon and taken into captivity. God used King Nebuchadnezzar to humble Israel and get the people to a place where they would eventually turn in repentance. Let's ponder a few circumstances that took place under Jeremiah the prophet: (1) Why did Jeremiah call the nation to repentance? (2) How did the nation respond? (3) What was the outcome of their response? (4) What caused God to bring awakening and restoration?

The Nation's Call to Repentance

God used the prophet Jeremiah in an attempt to get the attention of Israel and turn the people from their sin. Israel had broken its covenant with God. The nation was practicing idolatry, in direct rebellion against the Ten Commandments Moses had given (see Exodus 20:4–6).[2]

Social injustice and religious ritualism were also indictments against the nation. God didn't promise Jeremiah popularity and prestige; rather, he was called "to uproot and tear down, to destroy and overthrow." God followed this by telling him in the same verse that he was also appointed "to build and to plant" (Jeremiah 1:10 NIV).

Many of the visions Jeremiah receives concerning Israel are not pleasant. One of them depicts a boiling pot tipped from the north, coming down and being on the brink of spilling boiling water upon the south. This was a prophetic warning of the coming Babylonian invasion, where Yahweh declared, "Their kings will come and set up their thrones in the entrance of the gates of Jerusalem" (Jeremiah 1:15 NIV). This was a clear warning that Jerusalem would fall to the Babylonians.

The Nation's Response

As Israel chases after other gods, God compares this nation to a wild female donkey in heat. Israel no longer recognizes or acknowledges its sin, nor even blushes in shame at its rebellious actions. In Judah's refusal to acknowledge sin, much less repent, Jeremiah prophesies horrific judgment from the hand of the Babylonians (see Jeremiah 4:4–6:30). God challenges Jeremiah to search the streets of Jerusalem to find just one righteous and honest person, and then He will forgive Jerusalem its sin. Nevertheless, Jeremiah comes up empty-handed (see Jeremiah 5:1–5).

Here, the idea of a remnant is introduced as Yahweh indicates that He will not destroy all of Israel (see Jeremiah 5:10, 18). The theological leaders of the day (prophets and priests) contrasted with Jeremiah, stating that the people were not sinning, and continually prophesying peace (see Jeremiah

6:13–15). In Jeremiah 7–10, the prophet zeros in on the seriousness of their idolatry, while they perform ongoing religious rituals as if they are in right standing with God. They mix the sacred and the secular, and explicitly intertwine the profane and the holy. The people are steeped in idolatry, while continuing to sacrifice to the Lord. This was in vain and deplorable to a holy God. Jeremiah 26 chronicles a sermon the prophet preaches that if the people would change and repent, if they would abandon idolatry and genuinely care for the widows and orphans, Yahweh would relent and they would avoid judgment. While walking in this gross sin, they had been expecting Yahweh to protect them. They were totally deceived. The leaders thought God would wink at their detestable practices. One thing is sure: God didn't wink at sin in their day, and He won't in our day either.

Jeremiah addresses arguably the most detestable sin one could commit, child sacrifice. He renounces the sin of Molech and Shemesh worship, the detestable gods of the Moabites and Ammonites, which were associated with child sacrifice. The people stooped to a horrific low where they built sacrificial sites and high places in Jerusalem where they sacrificed their children. Jeremiah goes on to prophecy that the next thing the nation will hear is wailing, the sound of judgment— all because they refused to listen to Yahweh, while instead listening to the lies of the false prophets (see Jeremiah 8:4–9:25). The false prophets are proclaiming, "No sword or famine will touch this land," yet they themselves will "perish by sword and famine" (Jeremiah 14:15 NIV; see also verses 14–18). God tells the people that they will fall dead because of all who participated in this reprehensible sin (see Jeremiah 7:30–34).

Jeremiah was a national hero. He was a bold, no-compromise man of God. He didn't care what anyone thought of him. I'd like to submit that this was a unique moment in Israel's history. Many nations of the West are now living in a unique moment of their own and have lost their ability even to blush at the vast immorality, abortion, and drug abuse. Their governments even legalize unrighteousness on a national level. Yet where is the outcry from the pulpit?

I'm not stating that a pastor or leader has to address the culture's spiritual bankruptcy and the decay of Judeo-Christian beliefs every Sunday. I'm not saying a pastor has to address the rise of gender-questioning in children every week, or give handles on how to live in a depraved culture. At the same time, however, there's a problem when a leader goes a year without giving a deep call to repentance or without giving instruction from God's Word concerning these national, social, and cultural surges.

I have never condoned negativity in a ministry or preacher. That isn't my heart in these statements. But the West isn't in a moment of "peace, peace." Cultures are shifting, and many pulpits act as if nothing is wrong. I am submitting that we must lift our voices because people in our churches are confused. We must be clear, as Jeremiah was in his day, and have times where we are clear and concise as to what the Bible says. We are heading toward judgment at an intense speed, and we need Jeremiahs and Nathans in our day, not just motivational speakers, encouragers, and new insights. All of this has its place, but not at the expense of prophetic warnings and repentance preaching.

We need clarion calls to holiness on some kind of regular basis—where our pulpits are gracious and loving, while at the same time declaring clearly and boldly that awakening and revival are in our future. If there is failure to release prophetic preaching and clarion calls, judgment is in our future instead. I don't like to say this, nor do I take any pleasure in it. But we see a precedent all throughout Scripture when nations turn from God and no longer heed His Word. His judgment is actually an act of grace and mercy to get their attention.

The Nation's Outcome

The prophecies Jeremiah continually proclaimed start coming to fruition. King Nebuchadnezzar and his army begin their campaign against Israel. Jeremiah warns the king and nation that if they fight, they will die. The only way they will be able to save themselves is to surrender (see Jeremiah 21:9). In the midst of the calamity and coming destruction, Jeremiah gives a glimmer of hope for the future. He states in Jeremiah 23:5 that God will indeed raise up a righteous "Branch" from the line of David who will do what is right and just.

Neither the leaders nor the people heed the continual warnings of Jeremiah. Due to their refusal to repent and turn back to God, King Nebuchadnezzar invades and lays siege to Jerusalem. In Jeremiah's attempt to flee, the guards believe he's trying to go to the Babylonians, and they capture and arrest him (see Jeremiah 37:11–16). King Zedekiah places him in custody. Jeremiah continues to prophesy that it is futile to fight because God has raised Babylon to judge Judah. After word gets back to King Zedekiah of Jeremiah's continual proclamation of judgment and destruction, Jeremiah is lowered into a muddy cistern to die (see Jeremiah 38:1–6). However, the attempt to terminate Jeremiah fails when a foreigner, Ebedmelech the Ethiopian, saves his life (see verses 7–13). King Zedekiah does not heed the continual warnings to surrender and is overrun by the Babylonians (see Jeremiah 39:1–2). Everyone who had opposed and persecuted Jeremiah falls by the sword, including Zedekiah's sons. Then Zedekiah is captured and taken into captivity. Due to the favor of God, Jeremiah is allowed to live in either Babylon or Judah.

The destruction of Jerusalem was horrific.[3] The city and the Solomonic temple were destroyed. This temple had been central to Israel's religious life for four centuries. All the landscape of Judah was completely decimated, after which no form of life could find it hospitable for living (see Jeremiah 32:42–44). The fall of Jerusalem to Rome in AD 70 wasn't the first time the Jews were left bereft of their central sanctuary.[4] The years 587–586 BC have also been described as the "templeless age."[5]

Ezekiel 11:16 (NIV) says, "For a little while [the time of exile] I have been a sanctuary for them in the countries where they have gone."[6] At least for certain Jews, life without the Temple was hardly imaginable. After the initial shock gradually waned, they gained coping mechanisms, and this brought about the Gospel of a permanent solution: faith in Jesus the Messiah. John 1:14 describes Jesus this way: "the Word became flesh and dwelt among us." Old Testament passages like Zechariah 2:1–10 and Ezekiel 37:27 and 43:7–9 pointed to a time when God would dwell among His people in a new Temple, the living Messiah.

For the Jewish people, a human-built sanctuary was a place that would represent the manifestation of God's presence, with the expectation that soon Jesus would replace this model and give them a permanent manifestation of the presence of God abiding with His people.[7] The tent structure God chose to dwell in was replaced by the permanent structure King Solomon built, and any culture could come to worship the Lord.

Isaiah 7:14 states, "Therefore the Lord himself will give you a sign. Behold, the virgin shall conceive and bear a son, and shall call his name Immanuel." This name meant "God with us." In addition, John records Jesus referring to His own body as the temple (see John 2:19–21). Even more, the curtain that shielded the inner room of the temple was torn in half at His death. Jesus accomplished what the temple in Jerusalem never could: God not only dwelt with His people, but in His people.

The apostle Paul wrote, "Do you not know that your body is a temple of the Holy Spirit within you . . . ?" (1 Corinthians

6:19; see also 3:16–17). He also uses the metaphor "body of Christ" to describe us in the Christian community (see 1 Corinthians 12:12–27). Throughout the biblical story, God dwelt with people through a temple, but now it is through us. Instead of people needing to travel far and wide to encounter God, they can find Him in the people of God.

At this time of the exile, however, the walls of Jerusalem were completely demolished, the king's palace and every residence were burned to the ground, and any building with any significance was totally destroyed (see 2 Kings 25:8–12; Jeremiah 39:8). The temple priests were taken captive, and many of them were executed (see 2 Kings 25:18–21).

The destruction of the temple cannot be overstated as far as being a constant reminder of the spiritual failures of all who survived.[8] Its absence continually spoke to the moral and religious collapse of the community itself. Once the exile was over, prophets like Haggai expressed that there would be zero hope for the normalization of Israel without the rebuilding of the temple. Haggai deemed it inconceivable for the temple to remain decimated and destroyed.

Here we find the horrific consequences of sin and disobeying the Word of the Lord. In God's mercy for the people, He raises up Jeremiah to be His mouthpiece, declaring that they must turn from their sins. But they refuse more times than we can count. They treat Jeremiah with disdain. He is persecuted, mistreated, marginalized, mocked, and eventually left for dead. The priests and kings are rebellious and sinful. The people are deceived and followed the deceptive words of leaders who were called to fear God, but instead are in rebellion.

Today, we experience Jesus' presence through the Holy Spirit dwelling within us. However, in Old Testament days, this was not an option. The people met with God in places of worship and in the temple. Now those were all gone, totally destroyed. Imagine Jesus not living in you. Imagine having nowhere to meet with Him and experience His presence. This is the equivalent of what the Israelites were facing. This magnitude of heartache would be unbearable, and now they would have to live with it for decades to come.

God Brings Awakening and Restoration

What would take place next? Would God leave the nation in this depraved state, enslaved by the Babylonians? Would those who stayed in the destroyed city ever see Jerusalem rebuilt? Would repentance ever take place for the sins the people had committed?

God then raised up Cyrus the Persian, who overthrew Babylon. Cyrus made a decree allowing the Jews to return to Jerusalem. More specifically, his edict was to allow the Jews to go to their homeland and rebuild the temple Nebuchadnezzar had destroyed. Many did return and began rebuilding the house of the Lord. However, their efforts were not sustained. They became distracted by other concerns and left the temple incomplete for years to come.

Nearly two decades passed with no work done on the temple. Jeremiah 3:16 says, "And when you have multiplied and been fruitful in the land, in those days, declares the LORD, they shall no more say, 'The ark of the covenant of the LORD.' It shall not come to mind or be remembered or missed; it shall not be made again." How could this be? The temple represented the dwelling place of the Lord. It was where the people connected with God. Yet they seemed unconcerned. It seems they had grown accustomed to living without the presence of the Lord. These weren't pagans. The Jews were God's set-apart, covenant people. Yet they didn't have any urgency about creating a place for Him to dwell among them.

The fact that the people didn't have a temple could be likened to a church not having the presence of the Lord on a Sunday morning. People come and see a few friends, hear a message, sing some songs, yet there is no real encounter with the Lord. No miracles take place, no one gets saved, the gifts of the Spirit are not on display, young people are bored out of their minds and never want to come back. This is a travesty—leaders and individuals going through the motions with no presence or encounter. This is the epitome of religion. How can a God follower go on with life without the presence of the Lord? That's where the people were then, and where many churches are today. Yet people go about their day-to-day life as if nothing is wrong, when everything is wrong.

The halting of the temple's rebuilding didn't please the Lord. Therefore, in a display of His grace, God raised up Haggai the prophet to speak to His people. Haggai makes it explicitly clear that he is not rendering his own word, but the very words of God: "The word of the LORD came through the prophet Haggai" (Haggai 1:1 NIV). He is showing that he is but God's mouthpiece. The people must understand that to disobey what Haggai will communicate is not to disregard his words, but the very words of God Almighty. Haggai makes it clear whom he is addressing—both Zerubbabel, who represents the political power installed by Persian authority to be governor of Judah, and Joshua, who represents religious authority as high priest.

Haggai also doesn't mince words. He speaks directly to the problem, relaying the word of the Lord: "Thus says the LORD of hosts: These people say the time has not yet come to rebuild the house of the LORD" (Haggai 1:2). The Lord is not impressed with their delay. He doesn't refer to them as "my people," but "these people." This communicates in a very direct manner His annoyance concerning their inaction. However, the people didn't view their inaction as apathy. They thought, *We'll eventually get to it.* They felt no urgency, even though construction had stopped nearly two decades prior and they didn't have any good reason for the stoppage.

Haggai addresses God's indignation head-on. He asks the Israelites the question, "Is it a time for you yourselves to dwell in your paneled houses, while this house lies in ruins?" (Haggai 1:4). He isn't trying to get information. This is an admonishment from the Lord. The question shows that the people were more concerned about their comfort and living than they were about the house of the Lord. They were content living in their houses, some very basic and some lavish, while God's house lay in shambles.

Haggai's statement shows a stark contrast between what he says to the people and what David once said to the prophet Nathan concerning the building of the temple: "Here I am, living in a house of cedar, while the ark of God remains in a tent" (2 Samuel 7:2 NIV). David was concerned about the discrepancy of his life of luxury and comfort, while the ark was kept in a tent. He had an inner conviction that this scenario wasn't right, and a burden to do something. He desired to rectify the disparity, while Haggai's audience would go on making excuses for their apathy.

What a contrast between David and the remnant. David shows concern for what God desires, and the remnant exemplifies selfishness and a careless attitude toward what God wanted. David gives thought and desires to put together a strategy, but these people are making their living situation better, and God is an afterthought. This has often been a pattern of God's people, concerning themselves with their wants and desires above His own. This attitude has surfaced in more than one occurrence throughout history, as well as in our modern day.

We could conclude that the Lord indeed shows His covenant faithfulness as He moves on the heart of King Cyrus to allow the Israelites to return to Jerusalem, with an explicit blessing to rebuild the temple. Yet the Jews don't reciprocate the kindness of God, or show appreciation. They simply neglect God's house, leaving it in ruins, and go about their lives. Their lack of action depicted their unconcern. Clearly, they cared more about their well-being and homes than about the Lord's house.

Haggai gives them a direct message: "Now, therefore, thus says the LORD of hosts: Consider your ways" (Haggai 1:5). The subject isn't their inner feeling toward God, but their actions. God was disturbed by their inaction, not their inner feelings. God expects action from His people. Due to their lack of effort and apathy toward God in rebuilding the temple, He speaks through the prophet and highlights what they are going through. Haggai makes it clear that the people are in an economic crisis. The resulting calamity and natural hunger are due to poor harvests. Their continual thirst confirms a lack of water. Their clothes are insufficient because they are always cold. A metaphor shows that they earn wages but are experiencing loss, as if they put their earnings in a pocket with holes. They can never get ahead (see v. 6).

The prophet then repeats himself and communicates that "This is what the LORD Almighty says: 'Give careful thought to your ways'" (v. 7 NIV). The Lord also gives them another directive: "Go up into the mountains and bring down timber and build my house," assuring them that if they follow His decree, He will "take pleasure in it and be honored" (v. 8 NIV). This underscores that their actions would glorify the Lord. He would be well pleased by their obedience.

The prophet goes on to make it clear that they are experiencing the judgment of God. It isn't a coincidence that they are in a drought, suffering a severe food shortage, with earnings evaporating and calamity upon them. God tells them very clearly that there is a cause-and-effect relationship between their economic misfortune and His house lying in ruins.

Judgment came because of their inaction over His house while they took action to fulfill what they wanted. His very own hand has been against them. The only way God would relent would be due to their direct repentance and a change of direction.

The question is, How would the people respond to such a direct word? Israel had a history of not always heeding the word of the Lord, specifically when Jeremiah prophetically called for change and repentance. How they respond to the words of the prophet Haggai will have a cause-and-effect relationship with how God will respond to them. If the people repent and change, God will bless their obedience. On the other hand, if they harden their hearts, His judgment will continue and very well might increase.

Haggai communicates what happens next. Thankfully, Zerubbabel, who serves as governor, and Joshua, the high priest, along with the entire remnant of the people, respond to the word of the Lord. In unison, they all repent and make a commitment to the work of the Lord. Their response doesn't come months or years later, but is immediate and decisive. This shows they believe Haggai is a *bona fide* spokesman of the Lord (see Haggai 1:12).

As I already noted, God referred to the remnant as "this people," and now they refer to God as "their God." The terminology of "the remnant" also shows a change in the way God viewed them.[9] This reversal in language shows that they view their identity as the people of God and have fresh confidence that Yahweh is indeed "their God" (Haggai 1:12).[10]

Haggai 1:1 made reference that the message was to Zerubbabel and Joshua, but clearly it was to everyone, according to the response. Although it was implicit, the people were included in Haggai's message. They are referred to as the "remnant of the people," and they also "feared the LORD" (v. 12). This is the only way to respond to the word of the

Lord. This shows their awe of God and their reverence for His words.

The most encouraging words people can hear and know is that God is with them. This remnant responded in a proper manner; therefore, God gives a promise that He will be with them in their endeavors. Haggai said explicitly as God's mouthpiece that the Lord was declaring, "I am with you" (Haggai 1:13). This reassured them of God's favor and presence because of other instances they would have been familiar with throughout Israel's history. Jacob was given the same assurance as he began his journey to Haran (see Genesis 28:15). Moses received the same affirmation at the burning bush (see Exodus 3:12). God told Joshua that He would be with him as the mantle of leadership passed to him from Moses (see Joshua 1:5). The same was said to David as he entered into covenant with the Lord, and to Jeremiah as he began his prophetic ministry (see 2 Samuel 7:9; Jeremiah 1:8).[11] This was sure to energize the remnant and the leadership to fulfill the work.

Haggai now makes it clear that the people weren't moved by charismatic preaching, dynamic leadership, or pristine articulation. The people's spirits were "stirred up" by the Lord (Haggai 1:14). Haggai was simply the conduit who released prophetic preaching. Yet at the end of the day, it was the Lord Himself who stirred up the leadership and remnant.

The verb *stir up* here depicts the imagery of sleepiness and slumber. In the same manner as one is aroused from sleep to go to work, these people were aroused to rebuild the house of the Lord, where they were previously absent. They are now awakened and attentive to the urgent task in front of them. In this passage, *stirred up* means "to rouse, awaken, set in motion," and is many times used to describe the empowering presence of God to enliven people to accomplish His work.[12] Haggai understands that this stirring is indeed a manifestation of God's empowering presence to awaken the people to action (see Haggai 1:14).[13]

What a glorious moment in the history of Israel. A time of judgment is coming to a close. Ever since the invasion of Babylon, the nation had been under some form of chastisement for many decades. From the time of the gross idolatry and child sacrifice in Jeremiah's day, no one listened. Now the people returned but were still walking in error. However, in God's grace and mercy, He sent yet another prophet to redirect them in the right way.

Prophetic Preaching: A Working Definition

As we delve into prophetic preaching, let me state that Haggai prophetically preached to the people of Israel. He said what God was saying. Prophetic preaching plays a role, along with prayer, that contributes heavily to revival and awakening. It was his preaching that revived a spiritually dormant people to action. It was his hearing the voice of God and relaying it to the people that revived a remnant. His preaching led to a spiritual revival and awakening to move this people into action and into becoming concerned with what concerned God. A forerunner to any revival or awakening is for a remnant to become concerned with what God is concerned over, and then do something about it.

Prophetic preaching can be viewed as hearing what God is saying in prayer and not diverting. It is always substantiated by God's Word. Even though ministers today don't fall under the same category as Old Testament prophets, they are still called to hear God and deliver what He is saying. That's a good working definition of prophetic preaching.

As in Jeremiah's time, when child sacrifice was taking place, we can easily find today a tie to the past and the same pattern of sin relating to abortion. Not to mention the passing of gay marriage and the legalization of transgender surgeries in so many Western nations. Yet where is the deafening outcry from the clergy?

I'm not in any way attempting to paint all of today's leaders in one broad stroke, but research shows that there is far more silence on national sin than you might realize. In 2014, George Barna did a survey asking pastors if they believed the Bible addresses key moral and social issues in our day. The data showed that 90 percent believe the Word of God addresses these issues. Barna posed a follow-up question to those same pastors, asking if they would address these biblical issues. Suddenly, the number dropped to under 10 percent.[14] This means that only one in ten pastors addresses these hot-button issues, even though they fully understand that the Bible speaks directly to them. The cultural and social issues of the day are not limited to, but include sexual sin, abortion, homosexuality, divorce without a biblical precedent, the love of money, and many other topics.

Dr. Michael Brown is not only a theologian and prolific author, but is also a highly regarded cultural communicator in our day and time. He commented further on this leadership silence in his *Consider This* video series. In an episode titled "Why Don't More Pastors Speak Out?" Dr. Brown said,

> What reasons did the pastors give for their silence? According to [George] Barna, "There are five factors that the vast majority of pastors turn to. Attendance, giving, number of programs, number of staff, and square footage." In other words, these leaders openly stated that they avoided the controversial issues of our day because, in Barna's words, "Controversy keeps people from being in the seats, controversy keeps people from giving money, from attending programs." Isn't this like selling your soul for popularity, or for money, or for influence?[15]

Isn't this following in the footsteps of the false prophets in Jeremiah's day, who capitulated to the culture in order to keep their position and financial security? When Jeremiah spoke, they watched how he largely was not received and became unpopular. It seems that leaders who remain silent concerning these issues, according to Barna, are more concerned about their well-being, financial status, and popularity than about standing up for clear biblical values.

Not only are a large number of leaders not addressing these critical issues, but there have also been entire denominations advocating for same-sex marriage and abortion. They have joined ranks with the false prophets, in a striking similarity to Jeremiah's day, by continually declaring that people have not sinned (see Jeremiah 6:13–15). What a travesty and outrage. Men and women who have been called to uphold the holy Word are now deceiving God's people and causing multitudes to walk straight into apostasy. Dr. Brown asked these telling questions in his video:

> Looking back on history, how do we feel about pastors and leaders who chose not to speak out during the days of slavery in America? Don't we question their integrity and their courage? Don't we wonder how they could have nothing to say in the light of such evil? What about those who had no problem with segregation, yet preached from the Scriptures every Sunday morning about God's love and God's goodness? Something just doesn't line up.[16]

Rev. Casey Shobe, of the Episcopal Church of the Transfiguration in Dallas, Texas, commented further in his online blog "Sins of Omission,"

> Looking at the holocaust during the rule of Hitler, many of the pastors remained silent as six million Jews were murdered.

One of the few pastors that spoke up was Dietrich Bonhoeffer. In a quote that is widely attributed to him, he says, "*Silence in the face of evil is itself evil. God will not hold us guiltless. Not to speak is to speak. Not to act is to act.*"[17]

Here's how Dr. Brown summarized this silence on sin in our day:

> It's true that pastors are not called to be politicians and that their main focus is teaching and preaching the Scriptures and ministering to the needs of their people. But their people live in a very real world, and they need answers to the great problems and issues of the day. And the Bible provides answers to those great issues. To fail to speak is to fail to equip. To fail to speak is to fail to protect. To fail to speak is to fail to love.[18]

This calls for people like Bonhoeffer, who made a stand and spoke out against the genocide and atrocities against humanity that were taking place. He was calling for repentance. He shows a great example of prophetic preaching. He was witnessing mass genocide in the nation of Germany, which happened to be against the Jews. He understood that the Bible is clear on murder. He spoke against this brutality in the face of evil. Bonhoeffer was a prophetic preacher. He wasn't known for his words of knowledge and wisdom, or for predicting future events such as who would become president. Yet he was a prophetic preacher. Prediction is not the qualification for prophetic preaching. A key qualification is delivering the word of the Lord to bring people and nations to repentance and right standing with God. One use of prophetic preaching is to bring nations and the Church into alignment before a holy God.

Haggai and Jeremiah were powerful examples of prophetic preaching. Jeremiah was persecuted and unheeded. However,

Haggai was received and accepted. The outcomes were strikingly different. The people didn't listen to Jeremiah, so they were persecuted, killed, and taken into captivity. The people who listened to Haggai and the Spirit of God stirring them received favor, lifted judgment, and an awakening in the remnant. In Haggai, we see a powerful truth and a cause-and-effect relationship between his preaching and the people's response. They listened to the word of the Lord and were awakened to action. Their repentance and turning to the Lord through Haggai's preaching led to an awakening among them to fulfill the purpose of God.

One thing is clear: repentance preaching in this modern day is not popular! Let's set the record straight concerning the preaching of repentance: It must be done through a broken heart filled with compassion. It must be done with a desire for redemption and not condemnation. It must be done from a contrite posture that desires restoration and not damnation. Any repentance preaching that doesn't possess these attributes doesn't exhibit the heart of God. Jeremiah has been called the "weeping prophet" because he couldn't watch Israel's condition any longer.[19] Professor and author J. Daniel Hays says in *The Message of the Prophets* that because the nation of Israel foolishly listened to lies rather than to the voice of Yahweh, what they heard next was wailing—the sound of judgment.[20] Jeremiah 13:17 revealed the painful impact of the weeping that would be done if they refused to listen because of their pride.[21] Jeremiah said he would shed many tears when Yahweh's flock was exiled and taken captive.[22]

The prophetic preachers of today must possess similar hearts filled with compassion, while also staying true to the warning message. The West is engaged in some of the same practices as in Jeremiah's day. In his day it was child sacrifice, but in our day it is abortion. Some abortions take place because a woman is concerned about changes to her body. Others take place to cover up an adulteress affair. Some are the result of a one-night stand or fornication, where the resulting child is an unplanned inconvenience. Some take place because the parents don't want to endure the financial strain, so they have the baby terminated. These are forms of idolatry and child sacrifice. Children are sacrificed at the altar of image. Children are sacrificed at the altar of adultery. Children are sacrificed at the altar of convenience. Children are sacrificed at the altar of finance. Shame on nations that allow this! Nations must repent, with each of us repenting of our national and personal sins.

Nations of the West are allowing hormone blockers to be given to children in an attempt to alter their gender. Some medical professionals are performing transgender surgeries. There must be an outcry of truth from the pulpits, followed by national and individual repentance.

Marriage is between a man and a woman (see Genesis 2:24; Matthew 19:4–6; 1 Corinthians 7:2, among so many other Scriptures). There must be repentance for all sins of immorality, both nationally and individually. This is not an *opinion*; it is directly from God's holy Word. If anyone has a problem with these statements, it is not with the preacher, a church denomination, or an individual believer. The problem is far more intense because it is directly with God. These statements are not something the Bible's writers conjured up, but are God's decree to humanity.

Repentance Is Crucial to Awakening

The prayer of repentance is crucial to any awakening or revival. There is power in repentance! Yet sometimes the call goes unheeded. Acts 7 gives Stephen's speech to the Sanhedrin, where he pleads for them to listen as he shares the Gospel in full, starting with the story of Abraham. He explains in verses 48–49 (NIV) that "the Most High does not live in houses made by human hands" because He made all things. Stephen then goes on to tell his listeners they are stiff-necked people whose hearts and ears are still uncircumcised . . . always resisting the Holy Spirit (see v. 51). As Stephen was being stoned to death, he prayed that the Lord would not hold their sins against them (see v. 60). His plea for their repentance was from a pure heart, only desiring to reconcile them to God.

Do you see the continuity from biblical times, with conditions quite similar to the United States of America and the West? Or perhaps to your nation, wherever you are from? Clearly, God is a God of love. However, Scripture also reveals that He is our Judge and a God of justice. The Word of God sets the precedent, not the Church or any nation. Our current culture has demonized some clergy who preach the full Word, while praising other clergy who don't.

God's will is that none should perish and that all would come to repentance (see 2 Peter 3:9). The Lord is slow in anger (see Exodus 34:6). God's nature is not to destroy and kill, but to bring life, and life more abundantly (see John 10:10). But with this being said, the Bible is very clear on a number of issues that are today being violated without any sense of conviction or care on people's part. And laws are being established to protect and promote unrighteousness and sin.

In Haggai, one finds God using prophetic preaching to bring awakening. God used His words to awaken people's hearts to action. They then began to fulfill the words of the prophet. Where they had been apathetic to God's decree, they were now engaged in the work of the Lord. This is a sincere sign of true awakening.

Prophetic preaching is one of God's methods to bring awakening, and people respond by turning to God in a prayer of repentance. When such unctionized preaching is released and received, it can be one of the catalytic forces for heaven-sent revival. When prayer goes before God, demons tremble. The combination of spirit-empowered preaching, prayer, and travail is a recipe for revival and awakening.

IGNITING PRAYER

Search my heart, O God. If there is any wicked way in me, please show me, and empower me to repent and overcome it. God, I repent for not being bold when and where you have called me to do so. God, I repent for not making righteous stands in the public square. Give me the boldness of Jeremiah. Amid a corrupt and sinful generation, empower me to stand up and speak up until the devil backs up and shuts up! Set me free from fear and what others may think of me. I pray that your view of me would be the only one that matters. In Jesus' name, Amen!

I Will No Longer Watch Passively from the Sidelines

The Power of Taking Action

A key reason awakening is often needed is for the purpose of restoration. Restoration isn't required, of course, if people are already awakened and alert to the plans of the Lord. Throughout Scripture, however, prayer plays a key role in awakening God's slumbering people to action. Prayer is also significant in His restorative process. In this chapter, we will discover prayer's all-important role in bringing restoration to the people of God. We will observe how awakening takes place when prayer takes center stage.

One thing about God that remains true to His nature and track record is that He doesn't change. In Malachi 3:6 (KJV), He tells us, "I am the LORD; I change not." One attribute also true to His nature is that He is a God of restoration who never ceases to fulfill His promises, no matter how long it may take. In the previous chapter, we looked at how the restoration of God's temple symbolized His presence and existence among His people. In this chapter, one element we will observe is how God awakened His people to participate in His restorative plan and purpose in rebuilding Jerusalem.

God's will throughout Old Testament history was that He would have a people and that they would have a place. We see this at the very conception of humanity. God wanted a relationship with humankind, and He gave them a place to abide. For Adam and Eve, it was the garden of Eden. Sin disrupted this plan, and God then put into motion a process where He would once again have a people, and they would have a place. The place would soon be described as the Promised Land. God would speak to Abraham about a city/place, confirm it to Moses, and conceive it through the leadership of Joshua. Through many ups and downs, and multiplied years between the promise and the manifestation, God's will would come to pass.

As we ascertained in the previous chapter, Israel sinned, broke covenant with God, and was taken into exile. The land of promise and its temple were destroyed. Yet this did not negate the will of God or His promise. God will have a people set apart, and they will have a place. In this process, the place would not change from Israel and Judah. God's will was to restore His promise so that His people would live in the very place of the promise made hundreds of years prior.

This attribute of God's restorative nature runs true beyond the Promised Land. In any awakening or revival, He always restores marriages, broken lives, broken hearts, broken health, and so much more. God is in the business of restoring and reviving individuals, which is why Galatians 6:1 tells believers to restore people who are caught in sin. Peter serves as a good case in point. Jesus foretold that Peter would deny Him three times (see John 13:36–38). Jesus told Peter specifically that upon his confession of Jesus as Christ, the Son of the living God, He would build His Church (see Matthew 16:13–18). He also told Peter, along with the other disciples, that they would move in the miraculous power of God (see Matthew 10:7–8). This included raising the dead, casting out demons, healing the sick, and preaching the Gospel. In the process of Peter fulfilling his call, at one point he walked away in brokenness and went back to fishing. However, after the resurrection Jesus went and found Peter. He not only found him, but fully restored him to the place he was called to (see John 21:15–25). This is one of the most beautiful moments of God's restorative heart in the Bible. It also points to a personal revival for Peter of his walk and call.

God not only restores those who are called into ministry; He also restores those who have fallen or walked away from the Lord. A good example of this is the parable of the prodigal son (see Luke 15:11–32). This parable depicts a son and a father, and there's nothing the son can do to break the fact that he is his father's son. Yet he walks away. He breaks his relationship with his father and does what is evil in his father's sight. When this son comes to his senses and repents, he is restored.

This son represents someone who is in a relationship with Jesus and walks away. The story reveals that even if a person falls back into willful sin and disobedience, we serve a God of restoration. He restores our salvation. The father in this story didn't make the son grovel or pay penance. The son didn't have to earn his way back into favor. He simply turned from the error of his ways, repented, and received full restoration. This household was not in a moment of revival, but then the son coming home released joy in the house and revived the family. Restoration is a common theme of awakening and revival and cannot be downplayed. It's a pillar that can be found in and around any move of God.

God is not only in the business of restoring people's call or salvation. He is also in the business of bringing restoration to broken relationships. We see this between Jacob and Esau, and between Paul and John Mark. Relationships that were once broken and in disrepair are now restored. This can be found in a broken marriage that seems irreparable. With repentance and forgiveness, we can see restoration over and over again. God restores health, finances, purpose, and a plethora of broken situations. He is a God of restoration.

The Place of Prayer in Restoration

One of the ways God brings restoration is through the place of prayer. Prayer plays a heavy role because it serves to awaken action in an individual. There is power in taking action. A vital reason something or someone needs to be awakened is due to becoming dormant, whether it's a church, leader, people, or nation falling into a place of slumber or sleep concerning God's objectives. Therefore, God raises up an individual to awaken those in slumber, which is His ultimate purpose. We don't need to be awakened if slumber or sleep hasn't set in.

This reminds me of something Pastor John Kilpatrick once told me. He said, "Make no mistake about it, revival (awakening) doesn't start with a denomination. Revival/awakening doesn't start with a church. God knows it doesn't start with a committee. It starts with a man. It starts with a woman. Never forget that."[1]

This statement is very true. We find it embodied in the life of Nehemiah, cupbearer to the Persian king Artaxerxes. Nehemiah is still living in a land not his own, while other Israelites had left exile and returned to Judah. However, some (including Nehemiah) had become comfortable living in exile due to the destruction of Israel and Judah at the hands of the Babylonian Empire. Nehemiah had yet to return.

Years earlier, after the rebuilding of the Temple, Ezra had been granted permission to begin the rebuilding of Jerusalem. However, the work had come to an abrupt halt due to persecution from Persia (see Ezra 4:24). Restoration had begun, but it was incomplete. Though over one hundred years had passed since the city's destruction, God would not negate His promise that His people would have a promised land flowing with milk and honey. At this point, Jerusalem was far from that. How would restoration come to fruition? Would it be through a charismatic leader known for his speaking ability? No! Would it be due to intellectual prowess? Wrong again! Would it come to fruition because of a new strategy or marketing campaign? Absolutely not!

Then how would God bring restoration? John Kilpatrick's words are embodied in the process. The kind of restoration needed would have to occur because the people were once again *awakened* and revived to God's will, plan, and purposes. And the process of revival and awakening always starts with someone before it begins with a multitude. Here's where it started for Nehemiah:

> Hanani, one of my brothers, came from Judah with some other men, and I questioned them about the Jewish remnant that had survived the exile, and also about Jerusalem.
>
> They said to me, "Those who survived the exile and are back in the province are in great trouble and disgrace. The wall of Jerusalem is broken down, and its gates have been burned with fire."
>
> When I heard these things, I sat down and wept. For some days I mourned and fasted and prayed before the God of heaven.
>
> Nehemiah 1:2–4 NIV

Nehemiah receives news that breaks his heart. Although the temple had been rebuilt after Haggai's prophetic address to the people, the city walls still lay in shambles.[2] The people's safety, food supply, and well-being were in a compromised position. Not to mention what bothered Nehemiah the most: the city of God lay in disgrace.

The blow Nehemiah felt was not only due to the destruction left by King Nebuchadnezzar, where he had destroyed and burned the city nearly one hundred forty years earlier,[3] but was also due to the failure of Ezra's attempt to rebuild the city (see Ezra 4:7–23).[4] The attempt to rebuild was squelched by King Artaxerxes through his "stop-work" order. The restoration of God's holy city was at a standstill. This empowered hostility around Jerusalem because the halt on the rebuilding had royal backing.[5] Therefore, the city still lay in ruins, and its gates were burned by fire. Yet many Scriptures declared God's desire to give His people a blessed land (see Genesis 12:7; Numbers 14:8; Judges 2:1).

You may wonder why Nehemiah is so saddened. Imagine for a moment being in his shoes. He is living in exile, and his homeland has been destroyed. The temple has been rebuilt, but the living conditions and safety of the people are compromised. Think of being exiled to a foreign land with a foreign language and foreign food. God's people hadn't exited Judah by their own choice, although their sin had paved the way for it. They had been overthrown by a hostile power. Allow your imagination to meditate on where your emotions would be if your ancestors' heritage had been destroyed and the attempt at restoration had failed. Nehemiah was devastated. Not only was this a tragedy regarding the well-being of God's chosen people, but His will for them to have a place and protection was also in disarray.

These facts are bad enough, yet they are compounded by the fact that Nehemiah, being a godly man, must have felt the reproach that this could bring on God's good name. The surrounding nations could think that God was unwilling to restore His own people. This reproach on God's good and righteous character was more than Nehemiah could bear.

When God's name is scorned and He doesn't receive the reverence He is due, awakening is needed. When a people don't long for His will to be accomplished, revival is needed. When a nation is satisfied living without His will being carried out, there's a desperate need for a fresh move of His Spirit. This is exactly where Israel found herself.

Scripture tells us the people were in "great trouble and disgrace" (Nehemiah 1:3 NIV). The narrator (believed by some scholars to be Ezra, and by others to be Nehemiah himself) doesn't define what the "great trouble" referred to, but it likely points to the discouragement the people were under because the effort to rebuild was stopped (Ezra 4:7–23).[6] Construction of the city came to an abrupt halt due to a letter from Rehum to King Artaxerxes that accused the Israelites of planning to avoid taxes upon the completion of the wall.[7]

Nehemiah's response to the news of the remnant being in disarray is compelling. What he does is just as compelling and powerful as what he does not do. He does not find the sharpest minds and form a think tank on how he should approach this horrific situation. He does not rely on a charismatic personality or articulation. (I will talk more in a moment about how mishandling his current situation could even lead to his death.) Nehemiah gives us a perfect model of how to handle dire situations. This cupbearer turns to prayer, like many who had gone before him. He does not follow the many other examples in Israel's checkered past of those who turned to means other than prayer and failed miserably.

The narrator explicitly communicates Nehemiah's response: "When I heard these things, I sat down and wept. For some days I mourned and fasted and prayed before the God of heaven" (Nehemiah 1:4 NIV). Nehemiah is deeply moved when he hears of this disgrace and the conditions of the people and city. Upon hearing the report, he is shaken to the core of his being. His emotions begin to reel, and he loses his composure and can no longer stand on his feet.

Have you ever had someone tell you that you need to sit down before receiving devastating news? Nehemiah didn't have any warning as he fell to his seat. This wasn't an emotional moment that lifted in a few hours or days. He was shaken for many days, which turned into weeks, and weeks then turned into months (see Nehemiah 2:1). His emotions turned to tears. He couldn't hold them back. Undoubtedly, these were cries people could hear. What he turns to at this moment is just as powerful as what he does not turn to. He begins to pray and turn his face to the Lord. He not only prays, but begins to fast. The power of fasting and prayer is unequalled when we are seeking the Lord for help and guidance.

Nehemiah's persistent prayer over several months shows his resilience.[8] Fasting, when combined with prayer, strengthens the force of one's intercession.[9] His action showed where his priorities lay, and contrasts his natural demeanor for swift, decisive action.[10] Part of the art of healthy prayer is causing a person to slow down long enough to hear God in a precise manner. This is remarkable behavior on Nehemiah's part:

And I said, "O LORD God of heaven, the great and awesome God who keeps covenant and steadfast love with those who love him and keep his commandments, let your ear be attentive and your eyes open, to hear the prayer of your servant that I now pray before you day and night for the people of Israel your servants, confessing the sins of the people of Israel, which we have sinned against you. Even I and my father's house have sinned. We have acted very corruptly against you and have not kept the commandments, the statutes, and the rules that you commanded your servant Moses. Remember the word that you commanded your servant Moses, saying, 'If you are unfaithful, I will scatter you among the peoples, but if you return to me and keep my commandments and do them, though your outcasts are in the uttermost parts of heaven, from there I will gather them and bring them to the place that I have chosen, to make my name dwell there.' They are your servants and your people, whom you have redeemed by your great power and by your strong hand. O Lord, let your ear be attentive to the prayer of your servant, and to the prayer of your servants who delight to fear your name, and give success to your servant today, and grant him mercy in the sight of this man."

Nehemiah 1:5–11

What Nehemiah says in his prayer shows his understanding of God and His Word. The opening remarks bind together the importance of following the instructions of the covenant, God's lovingkindness, and each individual's love for God. This connection implicitly shows that people only receive covenant blessing as they walk out their love for God in keeping His covenant. This is a two-way relationship between God and His people. They cannot think that they can live a lifestyle contrary to the covenant, and sin as if nothing happened, while simultaneously expecting God to release covenantal blessing. Deep repentance on behalf of the people and the leadership was called for.

There is much more than a well-articulated and theological opening behind Nehemiah's prayer. He intentionally postpones a plea for help and never plays the card of victimization. In this way, he highlights that the real problem is not gates burned with fire or a broken-down wall. The actual issue and primary cause of their trouble is sin. He doesn't just reflect on God's loving and steadfast character, but also shows

God's majesty, which puts all humanity in its rightful place. In remembering God's covenant, he has raised the need for a personal response. This leads Nehemiah to a place where he must search his heart. Here, he owns both his personal and the national guilt. Nehemiah could have in mind 2 Chronicles 7:14–15 as he prays.[11]

The narrator opens the window by describing the intensity of Nehemiah's prayer. He is praying night and day, continually confessing sin as he prays in a manner that doesn't cease. Prayer is his chief activity. His life is consumed by a constant state of prayer. He isn't leaning into an educated strategy or bringing together a round table of like-minded individuals to find a resolution. He is absorbed with fasting and prayer as the only avenue that will bear fruit and resolve the situation. He understands the specific place Israel has found herself in, and he understands that it will take the action of God, and God alone, to receive a breakthrough and resolve the situation.

Nehemiah is now awakened to the dire need. He is no longer content just to serve the king wine. He isn't a priest or a Levite. He's a layman, secularly employed. Yet through being educated about the dire need and through prayer, Nehemiah receives a personal awakening. You don't have to be in full-time ministry to receive a personal epiphany for a specific mission, whether it be small or of great significance.

An Awakening Will Require Action

Note this: *an awakening will require action*. Never think prayer is not action. Praying is Nehemiah's first point of action. Yet it is rarely, if ever, the only action. Prayer is most often followed by a step to take, once God gives direction. Cooperating with God once the direction was given was key to Nehemiah's awakening—and is key to any other awakening, for that manner.

He comes empty-handed into the presence of the king, but is ready to make a bold request.[12] He understands the promises and threats of God's Word and doesn't come with a reserved plea. His prayer draws on a significant passage, Deuteronomy 9:29, where Moses made intercession to God: "For they are your people and your heritage, whom you brought out by your great power and by your outstretched arm." Nehemiah uses the same language Moses used when he pled for Israel on Mount Saini. The context of Moses' petition was that the people had made a golden calf and worshiped it, a rebellious act. God wanted to destroy them and start over. Moses made intercession for the people, and God showed mercy (see Deuteronomy 9:13–29). Nehemiah saw his current reality along the same lines as Moses' while he stood in the gap to avert the people's extinction. Nehemiah viewed his intercession as similar. His use of this kind of language shows the magnitude of the burden he felt and carried.

Nehemiah 1:7 states, "We have acted very corruptly." The New International Version states this as "acted very wickedly." The meaning of acting wickedly in Job 34:31 is to "offend." This shows that Nehemiah is communicating to God by approaching Him as a Master offended over the disregard of His commands.[13] Another facet that some rabbis hold to involves a more technical manner that sets the tone of taking collateral for debts owed.[14] This view shows that Israel must pay her debts, and if she declines, God will hold her most valued possessions, the land and the temple. Yet upon her repentance, these are returned to her. One can conclude that Israel was under God's judgment due to sin. The only way to reverse this would be genuine repentance. This was the action God desired in order to bring restoration and blessing to His people. Repentance is part of the beauty of Nehemiah's prayer. He is owning and repenting for the sin of Israel, the sin of his family, and his very own transgressions.

Nehemiah calls upon God to "remember" the very words He had given to Moses. Here, Nehemiah isn't just using emotionally charged articulation; he is also reminding God of His Word and praying according to the promise and statute God holds true. When praying in this manner, aligning with the attributes found in God's Word, we find ourselves in the right position before God. Praying His promises in the right circumstance is a powerful combination. This is exactly where Nehemiah finds himself. Nehemiah reminds God that He had promised to restore Israel upon their repentance (see Leviticus 26:40–46; Deuteronomy 4:27–31).

Even though many Jews had returned to Jerusalem nearly one hundred years earlier, after the Babylonian exile much of the city was in distress. The stop-work order had set the people back and placed them at a considerable disadvantage. This made the city vulnerable to attack and vandalism. It's likely that upon the stop-work order, much of the progress was, in fact, destroyed by vandals. Nehemiah desires for God to hear his prayer and reverse these dire circumstances.

Nehemiah gives God one last reminder that the Israelites are "your servants and your people," the nation delivered from Egyptian bondage through the power of "your strong hand" (Nehemiah 1:10). He is implying that God should have mercy on the people He calls His own and maintain the covenant relationship with the ones He set free from Egyptian bondage. One can see Nehemiah's plea for God to relent and bring restoration as a definite theme of his prayer.

With one last burst of emotion, Nehemiah asks God to listen once again to his prayer. He is explicitly asking for divine intervention and favor when he approaches the king. We should not think that his cry for favor with the king wasn't part of his day-and-night prayer that included cries of repentance. He plans to ask the king for favor in allowing the rebuilding of Jerusalem to continue, which entails rebuilding its wall.

Risking It All to Take Action

The reason for Nehemiah's petition before God to find favor with the king incorporates more than the reconstruction of Jerusalem's wall. If he doesn't find favor when he approaches King Artaxerxes, it could cost him his life. His position as cupbearer gave him frequent access to the king. His duty wasn't just to serve him the wine, but also to taste it to ensure that it wasn't poisoned. Then it could be presented to the king. Nehemiah's position gave him a significant level of influence with this ruler. To acknowledge that he was cupbearer to the king at this time in history acknowledges that God was already working on Israel's behalf. Yet at the same time, this scenario of petitioning the king tormented Nehemiah because if he mishandled it, he could die (similar to Esther's scenario in Esther 4:9–14).

Nehemiah was sobered by the fact that King Artaxerxes was the very king who had ordered the stop-work edict (see Ezra 4:21). Artaxerxes was still the ruler. This is the individual whom Nehemiah is about to ask for help. His request could come off as bringing a challenge to the king's previous ruling. This had the potential to go wrong in more ways than one. Nehemiah needed divine intervention from God, and he knew it. Therefore, he humbly came before God in fasting and prayer day and night in his plea for divine mercy and wisdom. Nehemiah didn't take the favor of God for granted as he approached Artaxerxes:

> In the month of Nisan, in the twentieth year of King Artaxerxes, when wine was before him, I took up the wine and gave it to the king. Now I had not been sad in his presence. And the king said to me, "Why is your face sad, seeing you are not sick? This is nothing but sadness of the heart." Then I was very much afraid. I said to the king, "Let the king live forever! Why should not my face be sad, when the city, the

place of my fathers' graves, lies in ruins, and its gates have been destroyed by fire?" Then the king said to me, "What are you requesting?" So I prayed to the God of heaven. And I said to the king, "If it pleases the king, and if your servant has found favor in your sight, that you send me to Judah, to the city of my fathers' graves, that I may rebuild it."

Nehemiah 2:1–5

The mention of the month *Nisan* (April) and the beginning of the Persian and Jewish year reveals how long Nehemiah persisted in fasting and prayer—around four months.[15] It was now time for action. Nothing can take the place of prayer. However, Nehemiah understood that action must also be taken. The hour had come. It is not hyperbole to say he was risking his life at this very moment. Like Esther, if he doesn't receive favor and offends the king, he could be executed within minutes (see Esther 4:15–17).

Note that this is likely the first time Nehemiah was ever sad in the presence of the king. This broke all etiquette. Servants were expected to keep their personal feeling to themselves. However, this was the day he had resolved to make his request known. Either his sadness was his calculated approach to opening the conversation, or he just couldn't hide it any longer. The moment was upon him, and the king asks him a direct question: "Why is your face sad, seeing you are not sick?" (Nehemiah 2:2).

If Nehemiah happens to mishandle his response, it could be his last. He understands that this question goes deeper than mere concern over having a bad day. Kings were always on the lookout for someone trying to assassinate them and were very suspicious of any activity out of the norm. The king was aware that poisoning through wine was a definite avenue for someone trying to kill him. Nehemiah isn't ignorant of any of this and understands that he is being directly probed by the king. This causes him great fear, and he will have to clear his name or face certain death.

Again, it cannot be overstated that this is why Nehemiah needed to seek God with the intensity that he did. He needed God's wisdom on what to say and how to say it in a manner the king would receive. God needed to lead and guide him at every turn because the gravity of the situation was dire. In such intense times, we need the guidance of God far above human reasoning or good communication.

Nehemiah responds to the king with honor and honesty. His answer shows his loyalty by his affirmation "Let the king live forever!" (Nehemiah 2:3). Next, he attempts to garner the king's help. He hopes the king will understand his burden and plight as he shares the deplorable conditions of the city where his ancestors lie. This was a direct approach to receiving empathy. Respect for ancestral tombs was universal among royalty, and Nehemiah's tactic carried the possibility of garnering the king's empathy.[16] In the ancient world, the deceased were not only revered, but worshiped.[17] When the dead weren't buried properly, they were thought to bring harm to those who didn't respect them. Nehemiah continued to lean into the king's recognition of this norm and was believing for a favorable response. This understanding would also show the urgency of his plea.

Wisely, he avoids bringing up Jerusalem due to the king's previous stop-work order. Yet at the same time, his straightforward answer resolves for the king that he isn't involved in a plot to kill him.[18] Nehemiah is being led by God. He does speak to the destruction of the city and its gates being burned with fire. However, his articulation ties the horror of the situation to the gravesites of his ancestors and implicitly shows that the people are vulnerable. Nehemiah articulating in this manner allows the king to save face.[19] This was not just human wisdom or ingenuity. God was leading and guiding the entire conversation.

Is the king offended that Nehemiah shared such a burden, knowing that he was the king who had caused the progress to cease? No, the king shows the exact opposite. He asks Nehemiah, "What are you requesting?" (Nehemiah 2:4).

How should Nehemiah answer? The king's question seems favorable, but Nehemiah isn't out of the woods yet. The narrator doesn't want the audience to forget that prayer is the center for Nehemiah in everything he has done, does, and will do. Nehemiah says, "So I prayed to the God of heaven" (v. 4). This could be taken as a quick prayer. Quick prayers can be effective if one has prayed sufficiently beforehand. This prayer, however, represents a life in constant communion with God.[20] Even though he has prayed for months, he knows he is dependent on God to intervene in this very moment. He answers the king with a request that he should be allowed to return and rebuild. More than likely, during Nehemiah's time in prayer God had spoken to him about leading such a mission. There is no evidence that he understood construction or had the skill set to take on this task. However, as the saying goes, God does not always call the equipped, but He equips those He calls.

When Nehemiah states, "If it pleases the king, and if your servant has found favor in your sight," he shows respect for Artaxerxes once again (v. 5). He is leaving it to the king to decide. There is genuine submission to the king's ultimate authority and wishes. Nehemiah exhibits an attitude of service and honor, not entitlement. Again, the four months of prayer had prepared him for what to say, how to say it, and the tone to use in saying it. This is evident in the dialogue he has with the king. Prayer gives us greater bandwidth to hear God in intricate detail, and this is exactly what Nehemiah needed.

In an explicit show of favor, the king asks Nehemiah, "How long will you be gone, and when will you return?" (v. 6). Nehemiah is prepared with an answer. If he had not had one, the king might not have released him. But after the king is given a time, it pleases him to release Nehemiah to fulfill this mission.

After Nehemiah knows that the favor of God and the king are with him, he begins to communicate exactly what he needs to fulfill the mission. He uses very honoring language and submits his plan of action to the king. He asks for letters that will ensure he can get to Judah without being detained by the authorities. He also asks that one of the letters be directed to the keeper of the forest so he can get the timber needed to complete the job (see vv. 7–8).

The king, in a monumental show of favor, grants Nehemiah everything he needs. In turn, Nehemiah recognizes immediately that "the good hand of my God was upon me" (v. 8). In his contribution *Ezra–Nehemiah* in the *Exegetical Commentary on the Old Testament*, Professor Gary V. Smith sums up all these events well by saying,

> The narrator emphasizes that Nehemiah did not achieve his desired response from the king by bribing him or any of his officials. He did not succeed because he was a master negotiator or knew how to broker a deal better than the king. His only advantage was that "God's good hand [was] upon me," guiding his thoughts and words (Nehemiah 2:8; Ezra 7:9; 8:18). The narrator believed that Nehemiah's months of humble prayer were key to his success (Nehemiah 1:4–11). Over these months, YHWH prepared Nehemiah and the king for this meeting, so that when the opportunity finally came, God graciously intervened to accomplish his will through both men.[21]

Nehemiah begins his mission with more than he requested: "Now the king had sent with me officers of the army and horsemen" (v. 9). It wasn't a lack of faith that he hadn't asked for this assistance in the first place. Rather, it could be taken that God does abundantly more than we can think or ask. God was providing everything he needed, even beyond his requests.

"Let's Rebuild the Wall!"

Nehemiah sets out to rebuild Jerusalem. He assumably arrives without incident, because no incidents are mentioned. He must now motivate the people to help. He couldn't take on this task on his own. How would the people respond?

> But now I said to them, "You know very well what trouble we are in. Jerusalem lies in ruins, and its gates have been destroyed by fire. Let us rebuild the wall of Jerusalem and end this disgrace!" Then I told them about how the gracious hand of God had been on me, and about my conversation with the king.
>
> They replied at once, "Yes, let's rebuild the wall!" So they began the good work.
>
> Nehemiah 2:17–18 NLT

It is clear by how Nehemiah communicates that the weight of his burden lies in the disgrace of the people rather than in their security.[22] The focal point of the people of God was Jerusalem, because it contained the temple. That the city lay in ruins could indicate that God was either powerless to help His people or unwilling. Both are poor reflections on God and are not true in the slightest. This being said, Nehemiah wanted to make sure the good name of God would not suffer reproach. That was at the center of his actions.

Nehemiah gives the people a proper perspective on their misfortunes and shows them that their newfound good fortune is because of God's favor (see Nehemiah 2:8; Ezra 7:6).[23] He communicates that it was God's good hand upon him that gave him favor with the king. The ultimate favor rests with God. The people's positive response is further confirmation to Nehemiah that he is in the center of God's will.

As Professor Smith further expressed, every single circumstance was God ordained.[24] None of this was luck, from Nehemiah meeting with his brother Hanani, to the king's approval, to his safe journey, and now to the people's enthusiasm to start. All these circumstances show God's activity. This wasn't coincidence, but divine providence.

God used Nehemiah to awaken a remnant to remove this disgrace. God used him to awaken the people after he was awakened. God never said it would be easy, however. Nehemiah and the rebuilders faced opposition over and over again and weren't celebrated by everyone. There were those who tried to intimidate, who threatened death, who frightened by a show of military force, who hired false prophets to prophesy against the people in order to deceive, and who falsely accused them of rebellion—namely Sanballat, Tobiah, and Geshem the Arab.

Through all the resistance, however, it's recorded that Nehemiah continued to pray. When opposition came through Sanballat and Tobiah, he didn't respond in fear or violence, but by praying in faith (see Nehemiah 4:4, 9; 6:14). The battle wasn't only won in prayer, but was also sustained by prayer. Nehemiah never moved away from a lifestyle of prayer. By God's grace, the people completed the wall (see Nehemiah 6:15). Prayer and action are deadly weapons against the schemes of the enemy, no matter what those schemes are.

Pray, Repent, Take Action

Nehemiah was living life to the fullest. He was serving the king and seemed to be well taken care of since Babylon had some of the best living conditions in the entire ancient world.

There is no mention of him carrying around a heavy burden or feeling the weight of God's people being in trouble. However, something changes the course of his life. He hears of the deplorable conditions of God's holy city and the rubble the people there were living in. Then as we saw, when he heard these things, he sat down and wept in compassion and grief.

This report moved Nehemiah to the core of his being. He wasn't a preacher or professional clergyman. He hadn't attended Bible school. He was secularly employed. But God needed someone, somewhere, to step up. He found Nehemiah. God isn't looking for the professional preachers in our day and time; He is looking for someone, somewhere, to hear the cry of a world gone mad and in desperate need of an awakening.

Nehemiah was moved by the dreadful condition of God's people and the fact that God's name wasn't being honored. What moves you? Really, ask yourself, *What am I moved by?* Nehemiah wasn't just moved for a moment, but for a lifetime. He didn't just have a flash of emotion and then let it die. It wasn't a stirring with a partial commitment lasting only a few weeks. It was imparted into his soul.

"*When I heard these things . . .*" I'd like to give you some hard facts that reveal how our world is in desperate need of an awakening. My prayer is that you won't simply read right through them, but will let God move you in the way Nehemiah allowed God to move him. Here are the statistics of my nation, where the spiritual walls are broken down, where the moral fabric of a society is lying in rubble, with gates scorched by fire. Your nation, if not America, will no doubt have its own broken walls and scorched gates. May this reality move you beyond a flash of emotion. According to the CDC, 40 percent of all children born inside the United States are born outside marriage.[25] According to Pew Research, in 1960 only 5 percent of all births occurred outside marriage. By 1970, this had doubled to 11 percent. Currently, it's around 40 percent.[26] When we view the world outside America, we see very similar statistics. In nearly every country, most children were being born within marriage in 1970, but by 2020, some countries (Chile, Costa Rica, Mexico, and Iceland) had reached 70 percent born outside marriage.[27] On a positive note, the countries of Israel, Malta, Turkey, Korea, and Japan still have the vast majority of children being born within marriage today.

When we consider the other countries seeing a major rise in babies born outside marriage, however, we see moral collapse across the board. The divorce rate in the United States has doubled from that of 1960, and statistically, 50 percent of all marriages now end in divorce or separation.[28] My country has the sixth-highest divorce rate in the world. Every 42 seconds, there is one divorce in America. That equates to 86 divorces per hour, 2,046 divorces per day, 14,364 divorces per week, and 746,971 divorces per year.[29] Why are people divorcing? Lack of commitment is cited 73 percent of the time, followed by arguing, infidelity, unrealistic expectations, etc.[30]

According to Pew Research, 59 percent of adults ages 18 to 44 in the United States have lived with an unmarried partner.[31] Young adults are particularly accepting of cohabitation, with 78 percent of those ages 18–29 saying it's acceptable.[32] From the early 1960s to the year 2020, the percentage of people living together has gone up dramatically, and it's now more common to cohabitate than to marry.[33] As recently as 2004, 61 percent of Americans were *opposed* to gay marriage.[34] However, Gallup found that nationwide public *support* for same-sex marriage reached 50 percent in 2011, 60 percent in 2015, and 70 percent in 2021.[35] According to the *New York Times*, same-sex couple households in the United States are up to 1.2 million, with 60 percent of those couples being married.[36] In 2021, a Gallup poll estimated that 0.3 percent of U.S. adults were married to a same-sex spouse before the 2015 *Obergefell* decision to legalize in all fifty states. In the first year after that ruling, the proportion of U.S. adults in same-sex marriages was up to 0.6 percent. According to one Gallup poll report, "Extrapolating those percentages to the U.S. population suggests that an estimated 1.5 million adults are married to a same-sex spouse, which would translate to about 750,000 same-sex marriages."[37] According to a U.S. Census Bureau analysis, 14.7 percent of same-sex couples have children in their household.[38] Outside of this is another 15–40 percent of LGBTQ individuals with children.[39] We must consider what this will look like down the road. NBCnews.com reported in 2019 that "The children of lesbian parents are less likely to identify as heterosexual as adults and much more likely to report same-sex attraction, according to a long-term study by the Williams Institute at the UCLA School of Law."[40]

"Reuters Investigates" and Komodo Health Inc. reported online that 42,167 youths were diagnosed in 2021 with gender dysphoria, which was nearly triple the number in 2017. This diagnosis was nonexistent until 2013, when it transitioned from being a disorder.[41] In the years spanning 2017 through 2021, the analysis found that at a minimum 121,882 children ages 6 to 17 were diagnosed. As a result, gender affirming care, including hormone therapy and surgery, have become optional. Medical treatments begin around ages 10 or 11, and over the last five years, there were at least 4,780 adolescents initiating puberty blocker treatments.[42] A "Reuters Investigates" article says this:

> After suppressing puberty, a child may pursue hormone treatments to initiate a puberty that aligns with their gender identity. Those for whom the opportunity to block puberty has already passed or who declined the option may also pursue hormone therapy.

At least 14,726 minors started hormone treatment with a prior gender dysphoria diagnosis from 2017 through 2021, according to the Komodo analysis.[43]

This same Reuters article goes on to state,

The Komodo analysis of insurance claims found 56 genital surgeries among patients ages 13 to 17 with a prior gender dysphoria diagnosis from 2019 to 2021. Among teens, "top surgery" to remove breasts is more common. In the three years ending in 2021, at least 776 mastectomies were performed in the United States on patients ages 13 to 17 with a gender dysphoria diagnosis. This tally does not include procedures that were paid for out of pocket.[44]

Kids are now having transgender surgeries performed on them. Some state legislatures are trying to pass laws that would allow schools to give kids hormone blockers without informing their parents. Prayer was removed from school in 1963, and we're now witnessing what is filling the void.

We see through these statistics the moral collapse of a nation. We could also note the mass school shootings, the vast increase in violence, the legalization of drugs, the number of abortions, and the disregard for basic law. All of this indicates one thing: *we are in desperate need of an awakening.*

Nehemiah sat down and wept at the crumbling of the physical walls of Jerusalem destroyed by the enemy. Even though they were natural walls, they carried very spiritual overtones. Such spiritual overtones are more explicit with our understanding of the current culture. Do you sit down and weep when you hear of the moral walls decimated and burned with fire by the enemy?

Nehemiah was educated about his current reality, and now we have discussed some of our current realities. Will you let

God break your heart with the very things that break His? Before the remnant was awakened and the walls were repaired, someone received a burden from the Lord. His first actions were prayer and intercession. Make a commitment right now that those will be your first actions as well.

Without prayer and intercession, there will be no awakening. The gates of hell will prevail. There will be no revival. With prayer and intercession, however, the Kingdom of God will advance, awakening will occur, the gates of hell will not prevail, the sick will be healed, and a nation will be restored.

It cannot be overstated: Nehemiah's first action was to go into an extended time of fasting and prayer, night and day. He repented of his sin and the nation's sin. He cried out to God for deliverance. What he did was just as powerful as what he did not do. Note that his main action was prayer. Prayer takes the discipline of patience. There are no quick fixes. There aren't any other means to rectify the situation. The same can be said about the West. There isn't a sharp think tank, a strategy session, or intelligence that will turn the tide of America and the West.

Nehemiah didn't jump up in haste; he waited in prayer. Others throughout Scripture turned to means other than waiting and praying. This caused more damage than good. Abraham didn't wait in prayer for God's promise of a son to be fulfilled. Sarai influenced him to sleep with Hagar, and that turned out to be a disaster (see Genesis 16). Aaron became impatient and listened to the people instead of waiting and taking the matter to prayer when Moses took so long to come down from the mountain. Instead, Aaron made an idol, and God was provoked to the point where He almost wiped out all the people (see Exodus 32). Yet those like Nehemiah, who understood the importance of waiting in prayer, witnessed the divine hand of God. Daniel, for example, experienced angelic deliverance after waiting and praying for three weeks (see Daniel 10).

The key for Nehemiah was that he prayed upon hearing the news. The key today is for us also to respond in prayer. A heartbreaking reality is that not doing anything can be almost as detrimental as explicitly doing the wrong thing. I will say with conviction that upon seeing the moral bankruptcy of society, to do nothing while the world is on fire is explicitly wrong. May God have mercy on the Church and every believer. May God awaken us to the place of prayer.

Nehemiah prays the prayer of repentance. Make no mistake—there will be no awakening without deep repentance. He repents over his sin and the sin of his nation. After four months of day-and-night prayer, his action turned into taking a risk and putting his life on the line in front of the king. In this hour, even though our main duty is to pray for awakening and repent before God, we must also take action. We can no longer stand by as spectators. We must speak out concerning these cultural atrocities and outright sins. We must have hearts of compassion and backbones of steel.

Yet when we do speak, we must also have on us what Nehemiah had: "the gracious hand of my God was on me" (Nehemiah 2:8 NIV). When Nehemiah spoke, the battle was won in prayer and the hand of God was upon him. This empowerment happens no other way than through the place of prayer. This should be our cry: *God, place your hand upon me in this depraved generation, to motivate your people to action and be a voice in the midst of corruption.*

What I am about to say is not hyperbole. If God judged nations throughout history for child sacrifice and for immorality and depravity, He will again judge nations who repeat these sins. God used Nehemiah to bring restoration to His people. If history is our guide, we have a small window in which to avert God's judgment. However, the good news is that we still can—through repentance and prayer.

You may say, "I'm not a professional preacher." Neither was Nehemiah. Yet he prayed until God's mighty hand rested upon him, and so can we. It isn't mystical or deep. You don't have to have a degree or ministry training. Begin to ask God to save your nation. Ask for His Spirit to be poured out. Cry out as part of God's holy remnant for Him to have mercy and spare America and the West. Cry out for Him to spare your nation, wherever you are from. As Nehemiah was used in bringing restoration through the action of prayer, God can use you.

It's time for a fresh wave of intercession to arise for awakening and revival. There is one hope: a God-sent awakening. It's revival or bust, awakening or judgment . . . if there is no turn toward God and repentance, what will become of us?

IGNITING PRAYER

I pray right now for the burden of the Lord to come upon me concerning the condition of my nation. I pray that a spirit of brokenness just like the one that fell upon Nehemiah would fall upon me now. I pray that it would not be a flash of emotion that then dies, but a deep, heartfelt burden.

God, in the same fashion as you put your hand on Nehemiah, put it on us. Not just for blessing and good feeling, but for mission that would empower our prayer and give us the anointing to stand up to the evil of our day and see the next Great Awakening. In Jesus' name, Amen!

I Will Not Be Moved by Dire Circumstances

The Power of Persistence

One observation we can make from the individuals referenced so far is that Hannah, Haggai, and Nehemiah not only prayed, but were persistent in their prayers. They didn't allow the obstacles or seemingly impossible situations to deter or hinder their heartfelt petition and cries. When situations appeared bleak and seemingly hopeless, these giants of faith courageously moved forward.

Jesus gives us a theology of prayer that has continuity with their persistence. He teaches the power of a made-up mind and inner determination that has settled on one key foundation: *I will put my trust in God and pray until a breakthrough.* This is a trait that not only plays a significant role in answered prayer, but is also a forerunner to any awakening. Revival history shows that from Azusa to the Hebrides revivals and beyond, fervent, unwavering prayer is key to any outpouring of the Spirit that will have a significant impact. Consider what Jesus taught about prayer in the parable of the widow and the unrighteous judge:

> And he told them a parable to the effect that they ought always to pray and not lose heart. He said, "In a certain city there was a judge who neither feared God nor respected man. And there was a widow in that city who kept coming to him and saying, 'Give me justice against my adversary.' For a while he refused, but afterward he said to himself, 'Though I neither fear God nor respect man, yet because this widow keeps bothering me, I will give her justice, so that she will not beat me down by her continual coming.'" And the Lord said, "Hear what the unrighteous judge says. And will not God give justice to his elect, who cry to him day and night? Will he delay long over them? I tell you, he will give justice to them speedily. Nevertheless, when the Son of Man comes, will he find faith on earth?"
>
> Luke 18:1–8

Luke gives us good information in his opening statement: "And he told them a parable to the effect that they ought always to pray and not lose heart." He explicitly tells his audience the exact intention of the parable Jesus will articulate. There is zero ambiguity. This parable is unlike many others Jesus told, where the disciples would have to try to figure out what He was communicating. In this parable, He made it plain.

Why did Jesus seemingly break here from the complexities of His teaching? Simple: He didn't want there to be any confusion. Prayer would be one of the most important aspects He would teach on. He didn't want His listeners to misunderstand or misinterpret these concepts, likely because of the circumstances they would soon face. Some would soon find themselves in prison or with death threats and persecution ever present. They would soon encounter trials and tribulations. He knew if there was one foundation that could not be off, it was the place of persistent prayer.

In this parable, Jesus teaches the people "that they ought always to pray and not lose heart," in the wording of the English Standard Version (which I have used as my main version throughout). Other translations enrich the meaning of this first statement. The Contemporary English Version renders this first verse "keep on praying and never give up." The Expanded Bible says that "they should always pray and never lose hope (become discouraged)." The King James Version adds that they "ought always to pray, and not to faint." Looking at the Greek in verse 1 of the New International Version, my Bible's study notes on Luke 18 translate *always* as at all times, and also as forever, constantly, and from now on. Looking at *give* in this context, the Greek defines it in my Bible's notes as giving up, becoming discouraged or weary, losing heart, and tiring of.

Jesus encourages His disciples not to quit, but His desire for them goes beyond simply not quitting. He exhorts them not to lose heart while praying. He exhorts them not to lose hope while praying. He exhorts them not to become weary or discouraged while praying. Jesus wants their hearts to be expectant and hope-filled in the process. This is a very encouraging word. He would not tell them this to get their hopes up just for them to be dashed. He knows that discouragement, hopelessness, weariness, and a desire to quit will try to attach to them. He wants them to keep their focus on Him and be encouraged in the process, even before they can see the breakthrough. Why does He say this to them? He knows there will be a time when they will be tempted to lose heart. He knows there will be a time when they consider quitting. He knows there will be a time when discouragement will try to worm its way in.

If Jesus knew these things would happen to the men and women who accompanied Him for three years, He also had you and me in mind. Have you ever felt discouraged in prayer? Have you ever wanted to quit praying? Have you ever begun to lose heart? Jesus isn't just talking to His disciples in this parable. He is speaking directly to you. No matter what the circumstances, or what the doctor said, put your eyes on Jesus and take His own words as encouragement. Don't lose heart, or become discouraged, or quit, no matter the temptation. This parable is for you to take heart and be encouraged. Jesus is cheering you on not to lose heart.

Jesus teaches His disciples to pray, continue praying, and not cease from praying. He wants them to learn that they should seek Him and not another in time of need. Even when God doesn't answer quickly or in what we would consider a timely fashion, we shouldn't waiver in our prayer.[1] Jesus wants the disciples to gain an understanding that it isn't the length of their petition, but the persistence that matters most; He wants His people to pray constantly and confidently: "they are to ask, seek, and persevere," expounds one commentary.[2] Jesus is clearly telling His disciples this parable to teach them that they should pray in a manner that never backs down, grows weary, or loses heart, and by no means ever quits.

To begin this parable, Jesus depicts two main characters: an unjust judge and a widow. As one commentary on the gospel of Luke points out, the cultural contrast between them is striking.[3] The judge represented the cultural elite, a male of privilege and power, and of noble status in this community. This judge was characterized in Luke 18:4 as someone who neither feared God nor respected people. This was the antithesis of how a judge was supposed to conduct himself. When Jehoshaphat appointed judges, he charged them, saying, "let the fear of the LORD be upon you" (2 Chronicles 19:7 KJV). He also charged them with orders to serve faithfully and wholeheartedly in the fear of the Lord (see v. 9).[4] The description Jesus gave for this judge as calloused and disdaining toward humanity makes it impossible for His second character in the parable, a powerless widow.

Imagine facing a judge like this. This individual was corrupt at face value. He didn't even care about the facts of the case. This wasn't an adversary the widow was taking to court; she was approaching a judge who was supposed to be just in his judgments. Widows, however, didn't have any intrinsic standing in the community.[5] They were the weakest of the weak. The fact that this widow, a woman in a man's world, kept coming to represent herself, tells us she didn't have a kinsman or male in her family to help her. It also reveals that she didn't have the economic resources to pay a bribe and receive justice. The pain of loss must have been unbearable. The voice of the enemy tempting her to give up, quit, and possibly end it may have weighed upon her day and night. Imagine the thoughts that likely raced through her mind as one rejection led to another, and another, and another: *No one loves you, not even the community of believers who are commanded to take care of you.*

In the context of Israel, this widow's position of being in a continual state of vulnerability showed the nation's depravity. The reason for her claim is unknown, but more than likely it had to do with material resources being held back from her. This widow was one of the most, if not the most, vulnerable in this society. She was alone. Jesus' original audience would have picked up on this immediately. The fact that there was no father, brother, nephew, or father-in-law to come to her aid shows how very alone she was. We also learn that she doesn't have a lawyer fighting alongside her. No advocate. No support. No comfort. She cannot afford a lawyer or a bribe. Where is the local community of believers? Where is her priest? Jesus is painting a picture of emotional, mental, and physical struggle against a judge who could not have cared less. This is an impossible situation in the natural.

Yet in the midst of dire circumstances, the tenacity and perseverance of this widow is remarkable. She was repeatedly slighted by the judge, yet continued to plead her case. She could easily have taken on the nature of a hopeless, helpless victim. Yet like the woman with the issue of blood who reached out to touch Jesus, she moved forward and didn't waiver or give up.

This is a shocking narrative as we consider the context. In this circumstance, a widow making this appeal would have had zero chance of success.[6] The culture she was in contrasted with the current culture of the West. Women in her era were of a lower class than males. They were at a disadvantage just because of their gender. This cannot be overlooked. Luke's audience would have picked up on the gravity of this fact instantaneously. Imagine a Jew in Nazi Germany facing a blatantly racist judge who disdained the Jewish race. A Westerner of today would underscore this as a hopeless situation for the Jew. The Jew would be deemed as having no chance whatsoever. Or think of a slave-owning judge in the early 1800s hearing a case concerning an African American slave. Not just a slave, but one facing charges from his or her owner. The slave would be facing an impossible situation, penniless, alone, and among the most vulnerable of society. Both the Jew and slave would need the miraculous intervention of God. This gives us a picture of the odds against this innocent widow.

His disciples certainly understood the impossible situation Jesus was placing this widow in. They realized that for this judge to grant her justice would be an act of God, a miracle. Jesus was teaching them that the kind of resistance she faced calls for more than just prayer; it calls for *persistent* prayer. There is power in persistence.

The Widows of Scripture

Theologian Richard Vinson contrasts this particular widow with other widows throughout Scripture.[7] Jesus has already shown the contrast between a grieving widow and a powerful centurion in Luke 7:1–17. In Luke 4:25–26, Jesus also commented on the way Elijah treated a widow. We could also look farther back, to Ruth 2:10–13, to see how a young widow approached Boaz:

> Then she fell on her face, bowing to the ground, and said to him, "Why have I found favor in your eyes, that you should take notice of me, since I am a foreigner?" . . . Then she said, "I have found favor in your eyes, my lord, for you have comforted me and spoken kindly to your servant, though I am not one of your servants."

Luke 18's widow is a stark contrast to Ruth. Vinson notes, "Luke's widow commands without any mollifying terms of address to show that she knows her place as a petitioner: 'Give me legal relief (lit., justify me, give me a favorable verdict) from my adversary!'"[8]

The main reason this widow acts differently from the other widows is because she understands the power of petitionary prayer. The reason she is so bold is that she understands the power of persistent prayer. The reason she is so tenacious is that she understands her position before God as an intercessor. This is one thing she possesses that is different from every other widow in the Bible whom we know of. There was something inside her that wouldn't waiver, cower, or shrink back. She was determined and made up her mind that she wouldn't be denied.

Due to the fact that he neither fears God nor cares about man, the judge initially continues denying her justice. However, she refuses to give up. She very well could have followed him and gone to his favorite places without a blush on her face, in tenacious faith. He is apparently pestered and harassed beyond what he can stand. According to one commentary, the language Luke uses comes from a boxing ring and depicts this frail widow punching this macho judge right in the face.[9] He doesn't oblige her because he fears God or cares about people's opinions, which he doesn't. It was only because of her relentless, unwavering pursuit because she would not be denied. Could this language of a boxing ring and this widow giving the judge a black eye be metaphoric language alluding to spiritual warfare? Perhaps it's what happens when people pray and petition God concerning injustice; they deal a spiritual blow to the enemy in spiritual warfare. The enemy metaphorically gets his brains beat in when a prayer for injustice or healing is answered.

At this point, we can see the clear contrast between this widow and the other widows. Why is she so much bolder? Why is she so much more tenacious? Why does she come across as so much more determined? Why is she so much more persistent? Simple! She understands the power of persistence. Her tenacious pursuit of the judge wasn't characteristic of a widow in her time; it was shockingly uncharacteristic. There is one reason for that: she held onto hope with tenacious grit.

As we read Jesus' parable about how we must pray and never lose heart, we may question, *How much more? How long?* Since this widow eventually received justice through an unjust judge, then it follows that children of God should pray with expectation that they will receive from a righteous and just God what they ask of Him. As Vinson writes, "We should then always pray—not with the mental image of nagging God into doing what we want, because God is not selfish or unconcerned like the judge. The 'always' has more to do with never giving into despair because of the world's injustice. One should not lose heart."[10]

The evidence shows that petitionary prayer has the power to overcome impossible situations and immovable obstacles. It also reveals that we must resolve not to lose heart. Our decision not to give up plays a powerful role in answered prayer.

We find through this process that although it seemed the widow was alone, she was not. Even though it seemed she didn't have an advocate, she most certainly did. Her advocate was none other than Jesus. Although her circumstances seemed impossible, they were not. Jesus was showing His disciples and everyone who would read this parable that no matter how impossible the circumstances are, nothing is impossible for God.

Not once did this widow play the victim card. Not once did she complain. Not once did she shrink back. No, she persevered! She is a lesson on the power of not placing our eye on the problem that we can see, but on Jesus, whom we cannot see. Through this allegorical parable of persistent and unwavering pursuit from the place of prayer, justice was granted to her. No matter where you find yourself at this moment, perhaps facing seemingly impossible circumstances such as sickness, addiction, financial catastrophe, relational turmoil, or depression, put your eyes on Jesus. You have an advocate! No matter what you feel or sense, make up your mind to persevere until a breakthrough. If God moved on behalf of this widow, He will do it for you.

If you are believing for awakening, press in and persevere. Yes, the circumstances are dire. Sin is normative throughout the land. Persecution is rising. Laws are being formed that protect evil and disdain the righteous. These are the times for which Jesus gave us this parable to stand on. Press in for a personal and national awakening. This is the time! This is the hour! It's not impossible. Put your eyes on Jesus, whom you cannot see, and through your persistent prayer He will change everything that you can see.

Like Nehemiah, what this widow did was just as powerful as what she did not do. It could be said that she did not let offense encapsulate her due to being alone, with no advocate. She also did not begin hating the judge due to the injustice. Offense, bitterness, and dishonor would have shut her prayer down, even with her persistence. Aspects like these can hinder our prayer, even if we are persistent.

Praying with Faith

In Mark 11, Jesus gives us another layer of insight into prayer that will complement what we found in Luke 18. Combining the truths of Luke 18 with the truths we will discover in Mark 11 has the potential to unlock powerful intercession that will produce a Great Awakening.

> And Jesus answered them, "Have faith in God. Truly, I say to you, whoever says to this mountain, 'Be taken up and thrown into the sea,' and does not doubt in his heart, but believes that what he says will come to pass, it will be done for him. Therefore I tell you, whatever you ask in prayer, believe that you have received it, and it will be yours. And whenever you stand praying, forgive, if you have anything against anyone, so that your Father also who is in heaven may forgive you your trespasses."
>
> Mark 11:22–25

One commentary writer on Mark's gospel points out that this passage has little to do with the cursing of the fig tree we find in verses 12–21, which comes before it. This is because the cursing of the fig tree has nothing to do with prayer, faith, or forgiveness, which is the theme of verses 22–25.[11] The expression used in verse 22, "faith in God," puts God as the object. The kind of faith God seeks is detailed in verses 23–25.

Another commentary writer points out that "Have faith in God" is commonly interpreted as an exhortation, but that it's plausible for it to be viewed as more of an encouragement than an exhortation, and that verses 23–24 "are grounded explicitly on God's faithfulness."[12] In this line of thought, the burden is not on the believer to somehow banish any presumption of doubt from his or her heart. The kind of faith Jesus calls for is confidence in the goodness and power of God, who accomplishes everything. Here, the natural consequence of faith is that God will indeed perform a miracle on one's behalf. Therefore, says this commentator, "in this immediate context, faith is unwavering trust in miraculous divine help."[13]

What an encouraging truth! What a freeing truth! What an uplifting truth! Many have interpreted this passage and put the weight of burden on the believer's ability to banish any doubt—implying that when we have 100 percent pure faith with zero doubt, our request will be granted. Here, the burden is not on the believer's perfected prayer. The burden on the believer is to put his or her trust in the attributes of God, by faith in prayer. Attributes such as *God is a healer!* Truths that show *God is a miracle-working God!* Facts that show *God is good!* Scriptures that prove *God is faithful!* That's the burden on the believer. Not to have faith that we have reached perfection before a request is granted. The believer just needs to put his or her trust in a good God who is in the business of having His children's best interests at heart (see Proverbs 3:11; Jeremiah 29:11; Romans 8:28).

Let that bring freedom to your prayer. As you pray for the sick, you come with an attitude that God is a healer. When you pray for restoration, you come with an attitude that God is a restorer. When you pray for the salvation of a loved one or friend, you come with an attitude that God is a Savior. Let's adjust our attitudes and put our faith in the good attributes of God for our foundation, not in the emotional state of thinking that when we feel the right amount of faith in prayer, we will be heard. Let's put our trust in God, who is able and will answer us according to His good nature. Psalm 103:8 (NIV) says, "The LORD is compassionate and gracious, slow to anger, abounding in love." Psalm 34:8 says, "Oh, taste and see that the LORD is good! Blessed is the man who takes refuge in him!" When we pray, we will taste His goodness. When we pray, we are actively taking refuge in His goodness.

Mark 11:23 says we can move mountains. Jesus is using metaphorical language that we should not interpret literally. One question that arises in studying this is, "What did Jesus and biblical authors mean when this kind of language is used?"[14] The answer is simple: they wanted to encourage believers in the importance of faith coupled with prayer.

In one commentary, Jesus' language here is described as proverbial.[15] Moving a mountain is humanly impossible, *but all things are possible with God* (see Zechariah 4:7; Matthew 19:26). The mountain has continuity with the unjust judge in Luke 18. Both were impossible situations. Both stories had an entity that didn't stand a chance. The widow couldn't move the judge in the natural, and a human couldn't speak to a mountain and have it physically lifted and thrown into the sea. They were both facing impossible situations. The common thread is that both the widow and the individual speaking to the mountain would need the miraculous intervention of God for what they were petitioning to come to pass.

In Mark 11:24, God is resolute in His readiness to respond to faith in prayer. "When prayer is the source of faith's power and the means of its strength, God's sovereignty is its only restriction," notes one commentator.[16] Verse 24 coincides pristinely with the statement Jesus makes in Mark 10:27: "With man it is impossible, but not with God. For all things are possible with God."

There is agreement that Mark 11:25 is under the influence of the Lord's Prayer.[17] Upon examination, we can conclude that if we expect to receive anything from God when praying, there must not be unresolved unforgiveness toward anyone. Forgiveness must be dealt to others if we expect to receive anything from God. The unforgiveness here appears to be an offense/sin that will short-circuit one's prayer of faith. Therefore, we can conclude that it is not only faith, but also forgiveness contributes to the efficiency of our prayers. "And whenever you stand praying, forgive, if you have anything against anyone, so that your Father also who is in heaven may forgive you your trespasses" (Mark 11:25). Here, the prayer of faith is tied to reconciliation in the believing community.

Both Mark 11:22–25 and Luke 18:1–8 affirm that we must have resolve concerning prayer. Mark adds another ingredient that will thwart productive prayer: unforgiveness. There is substantial evidence that even if believers pray and petition while incorporating great faith, their prayers will be hindered greatly by unforgiveness. Therefore, as a pattern of prayer, we must practice continual forgiveness mixed with faith and petition.

Looking at the mountain and the unjust judge, we see an immovable object. An impossible situation. An unchangeable circumstance. An obstacle no one can get around. The widow and the individual speaking to the mountain are facing impossible circumstances. You can place yourself in their shoes. What's your mountain? What's your impossible situation? What circumstance are you facing that cannot be moved?

For some, it's an incurable diagnosis. For others, it could be a relational situation broken beyond repair. There are some in such financial peril that the loss of everything is imminent. There are others held in bondage by an addiction for years, if not decades. Or perhaps a family member or friend is away from God and is bound by many strongholds in the form of gambling, or drugs and alcohol, or immorality, greed, a false religion, atheism, or a plethora of other bondages.

These are all mountains that, to the natural eye, represent impossibilities. Yet these are the very situations Jesus was referring to in both these parables—situations that are absolutely impossible without the divine intervention of God. Here is good news: with God, the mountain will move, and the unjust judge will relent. In response to unwavering, persistent prayer that puts faith in a good God, God Himself will hear from heaven and answer. God will intervene with a miracle. The mountain of drug addiction will be cast into the sea. The mountain of cancer can be healed. The mountain of irreconcilable marriage problems will be leveled. The mountain of financial collapse can turn around. Whatever your mountain is, God can and will intervene.

As both these parables allude to, we cannot put our eyes on the mountain or injustice. Our eyes must be set upon the Lord: "So we fix our eyes not on what is seen, but on what is unseen, since what is seen is temporary, but what is unseen is eternal" (2 Corinthians 4:18 NIV). Therefore, we must anchor our faith in God, whom we cannot physically see, rather than the bondage we can see. The sickness, addiction, relational issues, and lost loved ones you can see are temporary. Fix your eyes not on those things, but on the God who can change, heal, deliver, restore, and set free.

Avoiding Offense and Unforgiveness

Before we move on, we must take one more look at a particular aspect in Mark 11:25: "And whenever you stand praying, forgive, if you have anything against anyone, so that your Father also who is in heaven may forgive you your trespasses." Even if you have your eyes in the right place and are persistent in prayer and putting faith in Jesus, there is something that can negate this powerful pattern: offense and unforgiveness.

The keys to breakthrough are evident. The keys to answered prayer are right in front of us. The keys to the miraculous are spelled out. However, just as important as what we need to do for breakthrough is what we must not do. Offense is in the same category as unforgiveness and will hinder not only prayer, but the moving of the Holy Spirit. We talked in chapter 2 about one occurrence where offense was a hindrance to healing, the time when Jesus healed the lame man lowered through the roof. The Pharisees were offended at the way Jesus spoke concerning the healing, and the only person healed was the lame man. Yet many translations, including the King James Version, of Luke 5:17, state that "the power of the Lord was present to heal them." The offense the Pharisees felt shut the anointing down and hindered everyone else in the room. So we can conclude that no matter how much faith people possess, unforgiveness and offense can greatly affect their prayers in a very negative way.

If you feel your prayers have been hindered, a good examination of yourself in the areas of offense and unforgiveness would be of great benefit. If offense and unforgiveness are present, make it right. Repent and ask God to help you. You may also need to go to the person involved and ask him or her to forgive you. This could make all the difference in receiving a breakthrough in prayer.

Harboring offense and unforgiveness can shut down the miraculous. A person can have faith to move the mountain, but if he or she holds offense and unforgiveness, the miraculous power of God will not flow through a vessel corroded with these negative characteristics. If someone has the faith to move the immovable, yet has unresolved relational issues with anyone else, these must be dealt with before obtaining a great prevailing faith heard by the Lord. Therefore, it is just as powerful to deal with all unresolved bitterness and unforgiveness as it is to pray in faith. We must deal with these issues so our persistent, faith-filled prayers won't be hindered.

Praying According to God's Will

Persistent prayer lined up with the will of God is an unstoppable force. Through it, the Kingdom of God will advance, and a Great Awakening will follow. "And this is the confidence that we have toward him, that if we ask anything according to his will he hears us. And if we know that he hears us in whatever we ask, we know that we have the requests that we have asked of him" (1 John 5:14–15). According to Professor Emeritus Howard Marshall in his commentary *The Epistles of John*, one thing that is clear concerning a believer's assurance of eternal life is his or her ability to approach God with confidence. To "hear" in this passage means to hear favorably.[18]

We can have confidence that God will answer the prayer of the believer. However, there is an attachment to God hearing one's prayer, writes Marshall. It must be according to God's will.[19] Marshall points out that even as Jesus prayed that the cup would pass from Him, He added, "Yet not what I will, but what you will" (Mark 14:36). Believers must apply this process in their prayers and pray according to God's will.

Prayer must be qualified "according to his will," notes another commentary author, Professor Robert Yarbrough.[20] Believers don't always know exactly what to pray for concerning others, or for themselves, for that matter. There are assurances that He indeed hears us, however, and if our prayer is according to His will, it shall be done. We are also taught about what not to pray. We should not pray out of selfish motives or for things that are sinful.

You may wonder why anyone should pray, if God's will is done either way. Yet asserting this would bring havoc on the free will God gave humankind. God desires and moves through human cooperation. It was God's will to set Israel free from Egyptian bondage, yet if Moses would not have followed God's lead and lifted his rod over the Red Sea, the story of deliverance might have ended differently and with causalities God never intended. Humans are human, and they don't always know exactly what to pray for. Gethsemane is a great example of this in the life of Jesus. As Yarbrough writes, "John's point is to affirm that we know God hears us when we request, not that we have unerring discernment as to what we should be requesting or how we should set about campaigning for it."[21]

Believers must pray in a manner of submitting to God's will and communicating, "Your will be done" (Matthew 6:10). As Marshall writes, "It is as we freely yield ourselves to God that he is able to accomplish His will through us and our prayers."[22] As believers pray, they make themselves powerful instruments God uses to accomplish His will. As we learn to pray what God wants, we will have our petitions answered in the process.

Romans 12:2 says, "Do not conform to the pattern of this world, but be transformed by the renewing of your mind. *Then* you will be able to test and approve what God's will is—his good, pleasing and perfect will" (NIV, emphasis added). Jesus also taught us to pray a specific way: "Your kingdom come, your will be done, on earth as it is in heaven" (Matthew 6:10). Theologian and prolific author J. I. Packer notes that Jesus is the Kingdom of God in person and that one must be "born again" to enter the Kingdom, but he also believes praying "*thy kingdom come*" looks to a new display of God renewing the Church, saving sinners, restraining evil, or bringing about good.[23] In fact, Packer says this section of the Lord's Prayer is "general intercession."[24] And to pray "*thy will be done*" means we deny ourselves and embrace a struggle with Satan. The

Greek for *be done,* in both Jesus' Gethsemane prayer and in the Lord's Prayer, means "to happen."[25]

Another facet concerning the overall context of 1 John 5:14–15 is that John has argued extensively throughout the letter that believers need to live without sin and that the blood of Jesus is a key part of the Gospel.[26] It is clear in verses 16–17 that we should pray for those who aren't living according to the apostolic teachings and are living in sin. Therefore, before John exhorts the believers to pray for their brothers and sisters in sin, he encourages them that God indeed hears them. We can conclude that prayers for those lost or living in sin are indeed prayers prayed according to God's will. If we pray according to God's will, He hears us, and 1 Thessalonians 4:3–5 (NIV) reminds us, "It is God's will that you should be sanctified: that you should avoid sexual immorality; that each of you should learn to control your own body in a way that is holy and honorable, not in passionate lust like the pagans, who do not know God."

The exhortation "he hears us" in 1 John 5:14 could mean that John's readers struggled to believe that God really heard their prayers. This would harken to James 1:6 and Mark 11:24, that one must not doubt that God hears one's prayer.

Additionally, humans should never put petitions in the driver's seat, says Professor Yarbrough.[27] Rather, he goes on, we should put the destiny of God's will as of the utmost importance, therefore partnering with Him in the coming of His Kingdom. The fulfillment of God's will is a common denominator Christ taught His disciples in the objective of prayer. Therefore, if God hears a person praying His will, it will be done concerning the petition, even if the petition isn't answered on the timetable of the petitioner.

"In any case," Professor Marshall adds to the discussion, "the point is that God's children can be certain of an answer when they pray according to God's will."[28] Mark 11:24 tells us,

"Therefore I tell you, whatever you ask in prayer, believe that you have received it, and it will be yours." We can ascertain many things from Scripture that are God's will. God desires to heal. God desires to save. God desires to set free. Therefore, when we pray such prayers, we have confidence that they are His will and that He hears us. It's not as clear-cut, however, when we pray for a certain car, house, or new job. These could indeed be God's will, but are not as clear-cut in Scripture.

James lays a clear foundation for what we need in order to receive from the Lord: faith.[29]

> But let him ask in faith, with no doubting, for the one who doubts is like a wave of the sea that is driven and tossed by the wind. For that person must not suppose that he will receive anything from the Lord; he is a double-minded man, unstable in all his ways.
>
> James 1:6–8

James also shows us how to ask, and how not to ask. Some believe James is turning to the thought of unanswered prayer. James is clear that we should ask of the Lord "in faith, with no doubting." He isn't speaking about conversion faith, but about ongoing faith—a faith that continues to trust in the nature and identity of God.

James doesn't mean that a believer may never experience a measure of uncertainty about whether or not something is God's will. Rather, he is condemning a lack of commitment, a divided loyalty, or an indecision or hesitancy that questions the integrity of God.[30] In this context, we shouldn't doubt the character of God, who gives freely and unflinchingly. To doubt His character would be to doubt who He claims to be. This line of thought has continuity with the gospel of Mark's understanding above. We should have faith in who God is and in His life-giving character and attributes.

Therefore, questioning God's good character is like "a wave of the sea that is driven and tossed by the wind" (James 1:6). This shows the constant instability, and not just in stormy times. It doesn't depict a tall wave crashing to the seashore, but describes the constant instability waves create. It suggests being caught in the constant up and downs and variations of the wind's direction and strength. This is a perfect depiction of the person who vacillates between trusting fully in God and giving Him allegiance, and not trusting. It depicts the person who cannot choose between the world and its sinful momentary pleasures, and submitting his or her life completely to God.

The warning in James 1:7, "that person must not suppose that he will receive anything from the Lord," wouldn't have been said if the doubting was just concerning a specific unanswered prayer or a gift not given. One commentary writer points out that the kind of doubter here is a fence-sitter—someone who hasn't given his or her whole heart to Christ; someone whose actions flow from a heart position being half in and half out.[31] This kind of person should not think to ever receive anything from God. James could be speaking of those who were contemplating following Christ, or those who had followed but were holding onto non-Christian habits. Says the same writer of such people, "They were attracted to Jesus the Christ, but were vacillating."[32]

James is dealing with a split heart in its allegiance to trusting God.[33] The double-minded person doesn't love God wholeheartedly, nor love his or her neighbor properly, and he or she doesn't live out the teachings of Jesus. The contrast to being double-minded is being single-minded toward God and His ways. This equates to receiving from God only with an undivided trust in Him—namely in who He is and in His goodness to His children.

A double-minded man is "unstable in all his ways" (James 1:8). James is depicting a divided heart/soul between the world and faith.[34] This seems to echo the words of Jesus in Matthew 6:24 that state no one can serve two masters. In Jesus' line of thinking, being double-minded would render someone useless for His Kingdom. This verse harkens back to the Old Testament concerning loving God with a united heart that remains undivided (see Deuteronomy 6:5, 13). There is a contrast here with the undivided heart and the heart that is hypocritical and not wholly devoted to the fear of God. The final phrase "in all his ways" show such people to be consistently inconsistent. This phrase illuminates to a greater degree who the doubter really is—persons who refuse to let go of the world and fully surrender to Christ. Such people are torn between obedience and sin, refusing to let go of the temporary pleasures of sin for the sake of discipleship. As one commentary says, "This description hit close to home in an age of nominal Christians who attended church from time to time, perhaps even regularly, but who refused to let God interfere with their daily lives and goals."[35]

Pertaining to "unstable in all his ways," the same commentary compares this to the person being a drunkard.[36] Drunkenness is antithetical to the word of God and could clearly be viewed as outright rebellion. This instability is compared with the instability of a drunk who stumbles around and is unable to steady himself, moving about and unable to go in a stable direction. These kinds of people are incapable of staying on the right path. This instability is painted by the picture of waves being tossed all over the place, with zero stability.

James teaches that one who lives a sinful life is double-minded and should not expect to receive anything from God. Consequently, living in this manner stifles one's prayers. We can conclude that sin causes people to be double-minded, and therefore their prayers are not offered in the proper manner and will be ineffective and go unanswered.

Persistent Prayer Births Awakenings

Turning our attention back to prayer that births awakenings, you can see from the evidence I have presented that determination and fortitude are prerequisites to seeing impossible situations rectified. To see God's miraculous intervention in hopeless circumstances, persistent prayer is required, without a predetermined timetable. If there was ever a time for the saints to persist in praying for awakening, that time is now.

We must also understand that doubt in the goodness of God must be removed. A perfect intercessor is not required to pray the perfect prayer. Perfect intercessors are not required to feel a certain emotion; they simply look to God instead of themselves. However, intercessors must put their faith in God and not doubt God's good character and attributes to heal, save, and deliver. Coupling persistence with faith in who God is creates a fierce combination in praying for awakening, or for any other matter. Jesus Himself prayed these types of prayers.

Praying persistent, faith-filled prayers in accordance with God's will releases an unstoppable force. It's safe to say that God desires all nations to walk in His presence and power, which embodies the essence of awakening. When we pray with unwavering persistence, believing that God will restore and awaken the nations, be assured that He hears us and that we are praying the will of the Lord.

A few things can hinder such prayer, however, as we talked about. Offense and unforgiveness will shut down persistent, faith-filled prayer concerning God's will. And as James communicated, so can continually vacillating between serving God and living in sin. This is a doubting person. Here, the doubter is not the person who has perfectly removed all ambiguity, but the individual who lives in sin, contrary to the will of God. This person shouldn't think he or she will receive anything from the Lord.

Therefore, the case can once again be made for an intercessor to repent continually. Repentance of sin is key to not living a double-minded life or harboring unforgiveness. As intercessors walk in repentance, pray with persistence, put their trust in God, and pray according to His will, they can be confident that God hears them and will answer.

Let's move forward with persistence, in faith that God hears us. No matter the mountains that stand in the way of awakening—whether immorality on a national scale, laws that protect evil, apostate denominations, national confusion of right and wrong, gender confusion, murder, or violence at an all-time high—we know God can move these immovable obstacles and bring a Great Awakening.

May we move forward with persistence, fortitude, and determination. If we do not grow weary, shrink back, or give up, we will see an awakening in this generation. Keep the faith, and rise up and pray. God is with us. No matter the timetable, may we believe until we see the nations as God's inheritance. God wants to bring entire nations into full-blown revival, but some of this is tied to our prayers that His Kingdom would come on earth as it is in heaven. All it takes is one remnant, no matter how small, to determine that God is going to use them until something shifts and awakening takes place.

Powerful Takeaways about Prayer

Developing a prayer life is essential to a believer's walk with Christ. For this reason, knowing how to pray is very important. We saw clear evidence in this chapter that teaches us how to pray, what to incorporate, and what could hinder prayer and make it ineffective. Here are five takeaways to help you develop your prayer life.

1. Pray with a mindset that does not give up.
2. When obstacles arise, like the metaphorical mountain in Mark 11, believe that you are praying to a miracle-working God and nothing is impossible for Him.
3. As you pray, search your heart so your prayers won't be hindered due to offenses or unforgiveness.
4. When you pray the will of God, you see your prayers fulfilled. Not praying for God's will results in an unfulfilled request.
5. If you live a lifestyle of sin, you shouldn't expect your prayers to be answered. Repentance, on the other hand, is a powerful and necessary precursor (or prerequisite) to effective prayer.

From these takeaways, we can conclude that we must pray with persistence and never give up. I cannot overstate the power of persistence! We must have faith that with God all things are possible, no matter how impossible things may seem. We must never harbor unforgiveness and have the expectation that God will answer our prayers if we do. We must understand that His will affects the outcome. And we must realize that sin can indeed nullify prayer, so we must live as intercessors with repentant hearts—hearts fully committed to God and to seeing His Kingdom come and His will be done on the earth.

IGNITING PRAYER

God, I ask you today to help me become more persistent in my prayer. Give me the inner fortitude that this dear, persistent widow possessed. Help me look at you and your attributes of being a healer, deliverer, and a good God, above any mountain that I face.

Jesus, show me right now where I am holding onto any unforgiveness. I am going to pause this very moment to reflect and to listen to you, so please help me identify any unforgiveness or offense I might have hidden in my heart.

Lord, help me release those people who have hurt me, so I can fully receive from you and so my prayers will not be hindered. In Jesus' name, Amen.

I Will Cooperate with the Holy Spirit

The Power of United Prayer
That Releases the Miraculous

The disciples found themselves in an antagonistic culture that stood against everything they valued. The environment was hostile toward the Gospel. They were in a place where they would become extinct unless God moved on their behalf. They would either impact and birth change in the culture or face incredible backlash. It was awakening or bust, revival or death.

Jesus gave these disciples His last words as He was about to ascend into heaven. This would be the last face-to-face address they would receive. His final declaration was imperative (not optional): "I am going to send you what my Father has promised; but stay in the city until you have been clothed with power from on high" (Luke 24:49 NIV). They were told to wait to be empowered by the Holy Spirit.

Luke starts the Acts of the Apostles with the same tone he ended his gospel of Luke with: "But you will receive power when the Holy Spirit comes on you; and you will be my witnesses in Jerusalem, and in all Judea and Samaria, and to the ends of the earth" (Acts 1:8 NIV). This was the moment and context in which Jesus would ascend into heaven (see Luke 24:50–53; Acts 1:9–11). The empowerment of the Holy Spirit through the place of prayer is the prerequisite for any move of God, cultural awakening, or revival, period.

Here, the disciples were left seemingly alone. Their Master had just departed. The climate and culture they were left in did not find them endearing in any shape, form, or fashion. The disciples were beyond grateful that God had raised Jesus from the dead, but they were left to birth the New Testament Church in the company of hostile individuals.

It's worth noting the historical and social context they would be thrust into as they sought to fulfill the commission Jesus left them with (see Matthew 28:19–20). Rome was in control of Jerusalem at this time, and the Romans were not friends of the Jews, let alone favorable to the newfound religion of Christianity that hailed another King who outranked Caesar. It was borderline treason under Greco-Roman rule to declare a king or lord above their emperor. The term *Greco-Roman* refers to the Greek and Roman philosophy of that time. The people were polytheistic, worshiping many gods and goddesses that they believed were involved in their lives. Yet the foundation of Christianity is this: *Jesus is Lord.* The Greek word *Lord* in this time period was mainly reserved for one person, Caesar. For all intents and purposes, Greco-Rome was a national cult with Caesar as its lord. Any Roman during that time would have been greatly offended by, and could quickly be provoked to violence by, someone claiming Jesus as Lord. The disciples would have to step out into this climate and proclaim a King, Jesus, who stood far above any earthly king, even the likes of Caesar.

As if these facts weren't bad enough, the reality that the disciples would proclaim a King who had hung on a cross was beyond the average Roman citizen's frame of understanding. Why anyone would ever want to follow someone disgraced to the point of dying on a cross was beyond their comprehension. The society was honor-based, and being dishonored through crucifixion and all it entailed was the most humiliating way to die. The cross was relegated to murderers and rapists. The humiliation of being stripped of one's clothes and hung exposed was considered utterly deplorable.

Now the disciples would have to convince this culture (or national cult) that its people should turn from their idolatry to follow Jesus as their King. It was inconceivable. It's beyond our Western frame of thinking to realize how detestable it would be for a Roman to follow someone who had been this humiliated. Their culture valued prestige and power. In their eyes, Jesus died in great weakness and depravity. Getting this cultural mindset to shift would be nothing short of a bona fide miracle in each person who turned to Jesus.

The Jews were not on the disciples' side either. They were just as responsible for having Jesus murdered as Rome. Jewish leaders believed Jesus was a heretic. They accused Him of blasphemy. Rabbis would interpret His followers' preaching as false and an absolute error against Scripture (see Matthew 26:65–66; Mark 14:63–64). Not to mention that the Jewish religious leaders were the very ones who conspired against Jesus and set Him up to be executed. If they did that to Jesus, they wouldn't think twice about doing it to the apostles. Therefore, both Greco-Rome and Jewish leadership stood in agreement that this newly formed religion was in no way to be followed, and to preach it meant putting one's life at risk for treason and/or blasphemy.

These were daunting circumstances. The atmosphere was hostile, violent, antagonistic, and opposed to everything the disciples knew as true. How would these followers respond? Would they push their best communicator forward to bring a convincing argument? Would they suggest that the brightest mind give an apologetic reason to show Jesus was King? Would they water down the message to make it more digestible? The answer is no!

The Answer Is Prayer

We can understandably conclude that the disciples' emotions were probably all over the place. The One they had given their lives to was now gone. These men and women had watched Him walk on water and raise the dead. They must have felt indestructible during those times. Countless people were healed of every incurable disease known to man, right in front of their eyes. Jesus spoke to storms, and they ceased. He told demons to flee, and they did.

Then Jesus is arrested, and they watch Him get crucified. Their morale must have fallen to an all-time low. Suddenly, He is raised from the dead. Now their emotions soar back to an all-time high. Then, before the euphoria has time to settle, He is being taken up before their eyes as He ascends into heaven (see Matthew 16:21; John 20:17; John 21:14).[1]

Going from the highest of highs to the lowest of lows, what would they do? They didn't develop a marketing plan. They didn't water down the message. They didn't form a think tank. They didn't rely on intellect. Luke tells us exactly what they did: "All these with one accord were devoting themselves to *prayer*, together with the women and Mary the mother of Jesus, and his brothers" (Acts 1:14, emphasis added). The New International Version states that they were "constantly in prayer."

Luke explicitly communicates to his audience of the time, and also of today, that prayer was the chief activity of everyone gathered in the room, including the apostles. This is Luke's first summary of Jesus' followers in the book of Acts, and the activity is none other than prayer. The apostles aren't concentrating on themselves or on the task they would fulfill, but on God, who would sustain their life and empower their mission.[2] These men and women were constantly in connection with God through the place of prayer. .

Through devotion to prayer, the Church positions herself to receive the Spirit.[3] Professor John B. Polhill depicts this Acts 1 verse under discussion masterfully:

> Verse 14 is often viewed as the first of the "summaries" in Acts, those passages where Luke gave a generalized review of the activity of the Christian community. The primary characteristic that marked their life together in this period was prayer, as they anticipated together the promised gift of the Spirit. Prayer was a hallmark of the church in its early days (1:24; 2:42; 3:1; 4:24; 6:6). The time before Pentecost was a time of waiting, a time spent in prayer for the promised Spirit and for the power to witness. There is no effective witness without the Spirit, and the way to spiritual empowerment is to wait in prayer.[4]

As they prayed and waited upon the Lord, the Holy Spirit was poured out upon all gathered in the Upper Room:

> When the day of Pentecost arrived, they were all together in one place. And suddenly there came from heaven a sound like a mighty rushing wind, and it filled the entire house where they were sitting. And divided tongues as of fire appeared to them and rested on each one of them. And they were all filled with the Holy Spirit and began to speak in other tongues as the Spirit gave them utterance.

Acts 2:1–4

What a historic day for the early Church. The heavens opened, and the Spirit was poured out. They all began to pray in tongues, and visible tongues of fire began to rest on every head.

There is continuity with Jesus and the apostles as they received the Spirit: both were praying at the time. Look at the moment when Jesus was filled with the Spirit:

> Now when all the people were baptized, and when Jesus also had been baptized and was praying, the heavens were opened, and the Holy Spirit descended on him in bodily form, like a dove; and a voice came from heaven, "You are my beloved Son, with you I am well pleased."
>
> Luke 3:21–22

Luke 4:1 proves this fact: "And Jesus, full of the Holy Spirit, returned from the Jordan and was led by the Spirit in the wilderness."

We witness a pattern here: When Jesus prayed, the heavens were opened and He received the Spirit. When the disciples prayed, the heavens were opened and they received the Spirit. There was a cause-and-effect relationship; the heavens opened up when they prayed. May this fact grip every follower of Christ. Jesus said, "Truly, truly, I say to you, whoever believes in me will also do the works that I do; and greater works than these will he do, because I am going to the Father" (John 14:12). Believers have the authority to do the works Jesus did, and even greater. When Jesus prayed, as well as His disciples, the heavens were opened.

May faith fill our hearts that the heavens will open as we pray. There was an open heaven not just in times of private prayer, but even as Jesus publicly prayed. May we experience prayer that opens the heavens everywhere—in our community, the store, a restaurant, or wherever we may go!

Devoted to United Prayer

When the apostles were filled with the Spirit after they prayed, they didn't just sit in the upper room and soak. God's presence must have been overwhelming, yet they didn't just remain there and relish in it. Everyone moved out from where they were, into the public square. They continued to speak in tongues outside, in public. This was a miraculous occurrence: "Now there were dwelling in Jerusalem Jews, devout men from every nation under heaven. And at this sound the multitude came together, and they were bewildered, because each one was hearing them speak in his own language" (Acts 2:5–6).

What did those listening hear? They exclaimed, "We hear them telling in our own tongues the mighty works of God" (v. 11). They didn't just hear eloquent speech in their own dialect. They heard something very specific. Everyone heard in their own language what God had done through the Lord Jesus Christ.[5] Specifically, what God had done through Jesus' life, crucifixion, resurrection, and ascension.[6] They were hearing the Gospel in a demonstration of God's miraculous power.

Those in the audience are beside themselves at this marvelous display of God's power: "And all were amazed and perplexed, saying to one another, 'What does this mean?' But others mocking said, 'They are filled with new wine'" (vv. 12–13). At this point, Peter stands up with the other disciples beside him and explains the baptism in the Spirit (see vv. 14–21). He then preaches the Gospel of Jesus Christ. After Peter's message, the listeners are cut to the heart and inquire how they should respond. Peter declares that there's no way to respond to the Gospel's message other than repentance, which entails total surrender to Jesus and a turning from one's sin and idolatry (see vv. 37–40). Yet around three thousand people gave their lives to Christ at that very moment (see v. 41).

What a marvelous birth of the New Testament Church. Jerusalem just got rocked by the power of God! Luke wastes no time in bringing attention back to the foundation of the early Church: "And they devoted themselves to the apostles' teaching and the fellowship, to the breaking of bread and the prayers" (v. 42). Observe that along with prayer, a few other items are listed for the Church to devote itself to—namely the apostles' teaching, fellowship, and the breaking of bread. Luke wants his audience, however, to *make no mistake*—prayer is at the heart of the early Church and the apostles. So they continued to devote themselves to prayer.

One commentator on Acts, professor and author Darrell Bock, observes that a community that prays is something Luke emphasizes concerning community life.[7] People of prayer show a dependence on God and a Church that seeks His direction, because God's people don't live by feelings and intuition, but by actively seeking His will and leading. Luke's use of the word *prayers* speaks to a range of praying, both set and spontaneous. The Jews were used to set times of prayer at the temple (see Acts 2:46; 3:1), and believers knew of the fixed prayer the Lord had taught His disciples (see Luke 11:2–4). Luke's reference to prayers here is broad in its scope, from spontaneous prayer to set times, fixed prayers, corporate prayer, and other styles of prayer. Luke wants us to understand that the early Church wasn't just a Church that had prayer meetings attached to its work; it was a Church whose chief and primary activity was indeed prayer. Prayer was the starting point, not something the believers sprinkled upon their mission. Mission develops from the place of prayer. The mission didn't create a thoughtful strategy and good ideas. It was prayer first, and then mission, and after mission, churches were birthed. What a glorious apostolic pattern.

As Luke continues his narrative in Acts, he shows his audience what the apostles' activities included, which was none other than prayer (see again Acts 3:1). Peter and John were men of prayer, and they were on their way to prayer when something miraculous happened that was directly connected to their prayer life, another miracle. Professor and prolific author Craig S. Keener says in his commentary on Acts,

> Luke often emphasizes dramatic divine interventions during prayer times. The ninth hour (3:00 PM) recurs as the time when the angel reveals God's message to Cornelius (Acts 10:3). In this case; the apostles were probably on their way to a co-operate prayer meeting in the temple (Acts 2:46).[8]

Keener also states,

> In this passage, it may be of interest that Peter and John are on their way to prayer (perhaps for their second hour that day) and ready to act before their afternoon prayers. Nevertheless, the entire context of Luke-Acts supports the frequent connection between prayer and divine activity.[9]

As Peter and John were headed to the temple to pray, a man who had been lame since birth and who had to be carried around received a miraculous healing (see Acts 3:2–10). This miracle wasn't done in private. Thousands of people were around as they gathered near the temple. The man who received the healing jumped up, began to walk for the first time in his life, and praised God. This drew the attention of thousands. All the people had witnessed him begging day after day in his crippled condition. The healing captivated them: "And they were filled with wonder and amazement at what had happened to him" (Acts 3:10).

As the people watched the miracle right before their very eyes, Luke describes once again their emotions: "While he clung to Peter and John, all the people, utterly astounded, ran together to them in the portico called Solomon's" (verse 11). When Peter saw the crowds, he didn't let this opportunity pass; he preached the Gospel. Whenever the apostles preached, they would include four main tenets. Luke records these in Peter's sermon. One tenet Peter proclaims is that Jesus is the Messiah.[10] He is Lord. Peter is proclaiming Christ's kingship, and the audience understands that kings require complete submission. This truth can often be lost in many Western world presentations of the Gospel, which can leave people misunderstanding who Jesus really is and what it means to serve Him as Lord and not just as the One who saves.

Second, Peter would preach the cross. The action Jesus took through His crucifixion was to redeem humankind from sin. Peter would clearly explain that Jesus was the substitute, the restitution for sin, and took our punishment.

Third, God raised Jesus from the dead. Without a resurrection, there is no salvation.

Fourth, Peter called for repentance and did more than just have people confess doctrinal truth. He called them to turn from their life of sin if they were to follow Jesus truly (see Acts 3:12–26).

A Pattern in Ministry

Here we can see an early pattern in Peter's ministry beginning to emerge. In similar fashion to Acts 2, when the people heard the miraculous proclamation about Jesus in their native language through Jews who didn't speak those languages, they now see a lame man walk, which is a bona fide miracle. Peter does the same thing he did in Acts 2; on the heels of a miracle, he preaches the Gospel. When he proclaims Jesus, it has a powerful impact and another two thousand are saved (see Acts 4:4).

Remember that this culture was hostile toward Jesus and the Gospel. For these individuals to commit to Christ was monumental in many ways. Believers would be persecuted and dishonored, which is enormous in an honor-based society. They would lose their jobs. Possible violence or death could befall them. Their children would be persecuted if they didn't bow to idols at school. There was nowhere to hide or fade into the background. Because of the contrast between idolatry and Judaism, being a Christian stood out and was counter to everything normative in the culture. Yet we can observe early indicators of a cultural awakening as God uses the disciples to shift and bring change as they push back the kingdom of darkness.

Of course, the religious leaders despised the preaching of the Gospel and jailed Peter and John. They ordered them to cease preaching that Jesus is Lord. They threatened them and let them go. The devil was furious, and preachers of the Gospel were at the top of his list. They would now face opposition throughout their ministry. They would face jail, beatings, and even death. They knew what was ahead of them, having witnessed firsthand what had happened to Jesus. They thoroughly understood what could be in store for them.

How would Peter and John respond to the threats after just being released from jail? Would they shrink back? Would they look to a new method? Would they lean on their intellect and develop a different strategy? Would they hire a marketing firm to help them with their image? No! None of the above. Luke shows us precisely what they did. It was a continuation of what they always did in the embryonic conception of the early Church—they *prayed* (see Acts 4:23–31).

The apostles began to pray for increased boldness of speech, not for their critics to be silenced. They cried out for courage to proclaim the Gospel without fear. They also prayed for similar signs and wonders to take place, like the healing of the lame man they had just experienced.

What was not included in their prayer was astonishing, given the threats they had received and their knowledge that they could face more than jail, and perhaps even death. Their prayer in Acts 4:24–28 contains a quote from the opening words of Psalm 2, which shows its divine origin:

> And when they heard it, they lifted their voices together to God and said, "Sovereign Lord, who made the heaven and the earth and the sea and everything in them, who through the mouth of our father David, your servant, said by the Holy Spirit,
>
> "'Why did the Gentiles rage, and the peoples plot in vain? The kings of the earth set themselves, and the rulers were gathered together, against the Lord and against his Anointed'—
>
> for truly in this city there were gathered together against your holy servant Jesus, whom you anointed, both Herod and Pontius Pilate, along with the Gentiles and the peoples of Israel, to do whatever your hand and your plan had predestined to take place."

Psalm 2 refers to Jesus as Yahweh's holy Messiah. In regard to this psalm's connection to their prayer, Professor F. F. Bruce stated in his commentary on Acts,

> The "Gentiles" rage against Jesus in the persons of the Romans who sentenced him to the cross and carried out the sentence; "the peoples" who plotted against him are (despite the plural) the Jews, or rather their rulers; the "kings" who set themselves in an array are represented by Herod Antipas tetrarch of Galilee in Paraea, while Pontius Pilate represents the "rulers."[11]

This shows that Peter's message, which details Jesus as the Messiah, is a bold proclamation. Peter is standing before the people as a prophet, speaking the revealed truth that the One they killed is not dead, and that this Jesus whom they crucified has performed this miracle of healing the lame man. There is no doubt that Peter is addressing the very ones who turned Jesus over to those who crucified and killed the Messiah.[12]

What tenacity and outright courage Peter employs. He rebukes the very decision makers of Jesus' crucifixion. The individuals who turned Him over to Pilate were standing right before him. How sobering is the thought of this moment? If they had killed Jesus, they could do the same to him. With astonishing fortitude, Peter rebukes them as a bona fide prophet would.

Instead of the rulers and elders killing both Peter and John, however, they release them. Where do these two go? A prayer meeting. Again, what they don't pray for is astonishing. They don't pray that God would remove all the opposition. They don't pray for safe passage. They don't pray that God would allow them to go somewhere else. They don't pray for favor with their adversaries. Instead, they pray that they would be bold—as if Peter's address could have gotten any bolder than it already was. They pray for God to stretch forth His hand and perform the miraculous (see Acts 4:21–30).

The manner in which Peter prays stands as an apostolic foundation in which he implicitly asks God that his request would serve as the pattern for the early Church. If it was a foundation for their time, it is foundational for the twenty-first century as well. What exactly does Peter have in mind to serve as the pattern moving forward? He remembers how they prayed, which led to Spirit empowerment. He remembers how God moved supernaturally through those preaching in the tongues of the audience's native language. He remembers God healing the lame man. He reflects on the fruit after the miraculous manifestation of tongues, followed by his proclamation of the Gospel, when three thousand responded and were gloriously saved. In Acts 3, the miracle was different but the pattern was the same, and two thousand were saved. Peter was praying to let this be the standard operating procedure of the Church.

What is that procedure? Constant prayer culminates in Spirit empowerment for a mission that releases God's miraculous hand. Spirit empowerment is also the power source Peter knows they will need in order to properly proclaim the Gospel. Spirit-empowered proclamation is imperative for transformation because it takes the message far beyond a comprehensive intellectual transfer of information that touches the mind and never penetrates the heart. This kind of Spirit-empowered preaching, garnered from the place of prayer, is the very ingredient that leads to mass salvation, with two thousand souls saved in this case.

Peter preaches after prayer and the miraculous, not the other way around. He preaches after the miracle produced through the place of prayer and God's outstretched hand. He is praying that God lets this be how the Church is built and sustained and moves forward. Make no mistake—this is how the Church today should operate. Prayer that births the miraculous, followed by earth-shaking, bold proclamation, brings in the harvest. This is indeed the pattern Peter is crying out for. May we cry out for this pattern again today!

Prayer and Proclamation

Observe that Peter's prayer was answered rather speedily. In Acts 5, Peter's shadow heals the sick (see vv. 14–16). This is directly connected to his specific prayer for signs and wonders in his Acts 4 prayer. His prayer yet again gave birth to the miraculous and emboldened Gospel proclamation. In his commentary on Acts, Dr. Eckhard J. Schnabel says that Acts 5:12, which states "The apostles performed many signs and wonders among the people," is an answer to Peter's prayer for signs, wonders, and boldness.[13] He also says that beyond healings, further signs and wonders aren't specified, but in light of Jesus' ministry, they would include exorcisms, nature miracles, and raising the dead (see Acts 5:16, 17–26; 8:7; 9:36–42; 12:6–17; 16:25–26; 19:12; 20:9–12; 28:1–16).[14]

Peter doesn't take long before he explicitly codifies the role of prayer, which will include proclamation. The Church experienced explosive growth, with more believers than ever being added to the Lord, both men and women. So many signs and wonders were done that people were being laid on mats in the streets so that at least Peter's shadow might fall on them as he passed by (see Acts 5:12–16). Imagine the administrative responsibilities that were forming. We can conclude that the apostles' attention was being pulled in many directions, including caring for a particular group of widows. Caring for widows isn't just a good thing; God requires it.

How would the apostles respond? Would they begin to personally administrate the food distribution to the widows? Would they start a building program to facilitate a feeding program? Some would say it was unwise not to begin to build and plan for more growth. Would they create a youth and children's ministry? Would they call for wisdom to slow down so they could catch up and rightly lead?

None of the above! They would declare and lay the foundation of their responsibilities then, and for the duration (see Acts 6:1–3). Peter would soon make clear the will of God for the apostles: "But we will devote ourselves to prayer and to the ministry of the word" (Acts 6:4). Professor Schnabel comments that the priority of preaching and teaching is preserved with this solution.[15] The apostles desire to remedy the lack of food distribution to the widows, while at the same time making sure that preaching, teaching, and praying are their highest priorities. Make no mistake about it—Peter explicitly states that the apostles will give all their energies to their top priorities, which are prayer, the word, and the preaching and teaching of the Gospel.

Peter is not asking the others; he is telling them that this is what their primary job description will entail. He doesn't say he will never visit individuals in the Church. He doesn't say future building maintenance is something he will never provide time for. He doesn't say he will never attend civic functions. He doesn't say he will never go to the ball game of someone in the Church. He says the apostles will refuse to wear themselves out with this kind of responsibility. They understand that they will stagnate Church growth if they give themselves mainly to these activities. Therefore, it's safe to say that what many in the West think helps Church growth actually negates it when placed against the apostolic model Peter gives credence to. The apostles will not and should not give themselves to social activities. They should give themselves to prayer and the proclamation of the Gospel. What would the communities of the West look like if the chief activity of local ministry leaders was prayer and proclamation? What would it look like if ministry leaders gave as much time to prayer as they do to administration? I submit that we would have what the early Church had—a cultural revolution.

The apostles provide a solution, and the people love it. They appoint men filled with the Spirit to take on these duties to the widows (see Acts 6:5–7). Here, we see the cement dry on the apostolic foundation of the early Church. It is a clear pattern from Acts 1–6. Prayer touches God in such a manner that He performs the miraculous, and at the same time, by the Holy Spirit, empowers the proclamation of the Gospel through the apostles' preaching, which in turn produces a mass harvest of souls. What a foundation!

It's more probable than not, writes Professor Schnabel, that Luke included this episode in his narrative of early Church history in order galvanize the audience not only in his own dispensation of time, but also in the twenty-first century, around the high importance of prayer and proclamation for a growing and authentic Church.[16] This pattern should be included in every church growth seminar anyone attends. Luke shows that not everything is equally important in the Church's activity, and that prayer and proclamation trump all other Church leadership activities. Schnabel goes on to state,

> The priority of church leaders is prayer. Speaking with God, whom one cannot see, is difficult. But prayer is a fundamental priority for church leaders. To refer to the entertainment culture of the West again, it is not surprising that many churches have given up on prayer meetings, and it is not surprising that "worship pastors" who want to have "fast paced" and "attractive" worship services often desperately minimize prayer, reducing praying to one-liners between songs. Praying is not entertaining. When we come into God's presence, the presence of God's Spirit helps us in our prayers (Romans 8:26–27). And it is not surprising that in countries where many believers are poor or persecuted, the prayers are long and fervent, persistent and extended.[17]

Luke doesn't stop with his motif of prayer in Acts. On the contrary, he gives more evidence that prayer and the miraculous go hand in hand. This is part of Luke's theology—first prayer, then the miraculous, followed by proclamation and mass salvation.

When the Pattern Is Right

After Peter lays the foundation of prayer, proclamation of the Gospel, and devotion to God's Word as the ultimate priority for Church leadership, people other than the apostles begin to flow in the miraculous. When the pattern is right, God's glory, presence, and power will follow. Now for the first time, two individuals not listed among the apostles begin to flow in signs and wonders, none other than Stephen and Philip.

Both are documented as moving in the miraculous. After prayer was laid as a cornerstone of the Church's leadership, the believers were released in a fresh wave of power, miracles, and fruitful proclamation (see Acts 6:8; Acts 8:6).

Stephen would be stoned for his preaching. During his execution, however, he offers a prayer for his accusers and for those who are carrying out his execution. One of them is none other than Saul of Tarsus. Later, on the road to Damascus, Saul would be visited by Jesus Himself, be struck blind, and fall to the ground. This was a miraculous encounter that directly answered Stephen's prayer for him. Prayer gave birth to Saul's miraculous encounter with Jesus, which confirmed the Gospel message proclaimed by Stephen.

Following his powerful encounter, Saul would receive Christ. He was then led away to a place where he would fast and pray, and he was given a word of knowledge about a man who would visit him. God was very specific with Saul and shared the very name of this individual (see Acts 9:9–12). Here again, we see a direct connection between prayer and the power of God. The man's name was Ananias. Luke calls him a disciple.

Earlier we saw Luke's description of the early Church as a people of prayer, so we know Ananias was a man of prayer (see Acts 2:42). Because he was a praying man, his heart was in the right place to hear from God. Not only did Saul get a word of knowledge, but Ananias also did. He was given the street and exact house where Saul was staying. This was a prolific word of knowledge. Once again, from the description of him as a disciple, we know it came directly out of Ananias's prayer life. Jesus tells him specifically what to do—lay hands on Saul so through this process Saul would receive his sight and be filled with the Holy Spirit (see Acts 9:10–16).

Ananias is nervous because he knows Saul has persecuted the Church. Jesus encourages him, and he goes forth, laying hands on Saul, seeing Saul's sight restored, and being used to see Saul filled with the Holy Spirit. Saul eats, is strengthened, and instantly begins to preach the Gospel (Acts 9:17–20).

Once again, we see explicitly that from Stephen's prayer to Saul's prayer to the prayer life of Ananias, the same pattern continues. Prayer gives birth to the miraculous and empowers proclamation that leads to salvation. As pastor and professor Tony Merida puts it in his commentary on Acts, this self-righteous persecutor of the Church is now transformed into a Christ-centered apostle. Merida says of Saul, "He is no longer corrupt but cleansed, no longer a church foe but part of the family. What grace!"[18]

Turning back to the ministry of Peter, God uses him to raise the dead. Luke explicitly says that Peter prayed and a girl was raised (see Acts 9:40). After this, he didn't just leave. He stayed, and many believed because he preached the Gospel to them as he stayed with them for many days (see Acts 9:42–43). We see here the pattern of prayer first and foremost once again.

Another example of this pattern comes from Acts 10, when Pentecost would come to the Gentiles. Cornelius, a God-fearing man, prayed continually (see vv. 1–2). Then he had a vision of the angel of the Lord, who told him his prayers and alms to the poor had become a memorial to God. The angel then also told him to send for Peter, and told him the city and exact house Peter was staying in. This is a profound gift of the Spirit on display, the word of knowledge and wisdom at work together. When the angel left, Cornelius sent men to request that Peter return with them to his house. Prayer is an explicit activity that gives birth to the miraculous, this time in the form of an angelic visitation (see Acts 10:3–8).

Where is Peter while the men are on the way to retrieve him? Luke puts him right in the middle of his devotion time, praying. He is on his roof and has a vision. Then as the men sent from Cornelius's house arrive, God speaks to Peter and tells him about these men and how he is to go with them. They set out the next day. When Peter arrives, he begins to preach the Gospel to Cornelius and his friends and relatives. Right in the middle of his sermon, they are baptized in the Holy Spirit and begin to speak in tongues, and all are gloriously saved.

Once again, prayer has given birth to the miraculous. Peter preaches out of the overflow of the activity of God, and an entire household comes to Christ (see Acts 10:17–48). Make no mistake about it—this is the apostolic pattern to win the world to Jesus.

Prioritizing the Place of Prayer

The evidence we've looked at shows that prayer was a fundamental part of the early Church. Our model to follow in the twenty-first century is the early Church, especially the believers' devotion to God through the place of prayer. Upon Jesus' ascension, the disciples, facing a hostile environment to establish the Church, prayed (see Acts 1:14.) When the time came to replace Judas, they prayed (see Acts 1:24–25). After the first Gospel proclamation, when the Church was established, the new community of believers devoted themselves to prayer (see Acts 2:42). After Peter and John were released from jail, they went to a prayer meeting (see Acts 4:23–24). Professor Schnabel states about prayer,

> If sustained prayer is eliminated from "worship services" on Sunday mornings because they are deemed unattractive for "seekers" who expect to be entertained, or awkward for churchgoers who expect to be guided through a fast-paced program, the risen Lord may well be knocking at the door—from the outside (Revelation 3:20). Many Churches in the affluent West

live in spiritual poverty, as demonstrated by the decline in prayer. Christians who do not pray regularly and consistently are a contradiction in terms—they deny what they profess, that they have been reconciled with God (with whom they do not want to spend time), that they follow in the steps of Jesus (who prayed), and that they have received the Holy Spirit (who is God's presence, which is experienced in prayer).[19]

He goes on to comment that it is telling how people will eagerly meet at their church to watch a major sporting event together, while that same church's prayer meetings have been abandoned. Believers who yearn to be in God's presence reserve time for prayer, which is also telling.[20]

In conclusion, it's crystal clear that Luke shows that the Holy Spirit empowers God's people through the place of prayer, and then miracles manifest through God's outstretched arm. Proclamation of the Gospel then takes place, followed by mass salvation. This being the case, why isn't there a greater burden placed on prayer as a normative activity within the local church today? Why do so many churches not have a single corporate prayer meeting? If churches do offer a prayer meeting, why only once a week or even once a month? According to one 2014 study, Americans spend an average of eight minutes per day in prayer.[21] According to Pew Research Center, only 55 percent of people pray at least daily (this is grouped for all religions), but this statistic didn't say how long this 55 percent prayed.[22] Outside this, another study found that only 50 percent of pastors pray an hour daily.[23]

One thing is clear from the statistic above: modern-day leaders in the West don't pray as much as the early Church's leadership. I'm not saying this should be rectified overnight, but a shift must take precedence in every leader's calendar. The Church didn't move forward by making sure everyone was cared for, although that's important. It didn't move forward because of stately buildings, good programs, or hosting excellent events. It moved forward because the leaders' chief activity was prayer, proclamation of the Gospel, and the Word. It moved forward because the top priority and activity of believers was none other than the place of prayer.

The early Church didn't grow by accident. Church growth didn't occur because of the leaders' many degrees or brilliant human strategy. Their main strategy was *prayer*. It wasn't an accident that miracles and unique occurrences took place. They were manifested by God through the place of prayer. Mass salvation was no accident. Peter preached a powerful Gospel message that challenged every cultural belief and called his listeners to repentance, to turn from idolatry, immorality, greed, selfishness, carnality, and many other things. He called for their complete surrender to Jesus. You would be hard-pressed to find much preaching in the Church of the West on utter abandonment and surrender. Little preaching on taking up the cross and following Christ. Few messages on dying to self. This kind of preaching took place after prayer and miracles that led to mass salvation.

To say this would not work today is to say that the apostles were wrong and that we are more intelligent than they were. This is not the case. They experienced a cultural shift and awakening through a simple pattern that started with prayer. What if church leadership prayed more than they administrated? I can tell you what would happen—another Great Awakening and revival would take place. I can tell you that miracles would be the norm. I can tell you that mass salvation would take place once again. I'm certain that if leaders sought God in fasting and prayer with the same amount of time they give to administration, we would have a revival in the West that would shake the world in two years maximum.

Perhaps you are reading this book and you don't serve as a leader in the Church or in full-time ministry. That's okay!

You're like Stephen, Phillip, and Ananias, who weren't professional ministers but had various similarities to the apostles. Take Ananias, for example. He was a man of prayer and wasn't in full-time ministry. Yet through the place of prayer, he had a vision where he was told exactly where Saul was and told to lay hands on him so his sight would be restored and he would be filled with the Holy Spirit. Ananias then steps out as he receives Saul's exact location in his vision. He goes to the location and lays hands on him, and Saul is completely healed and filled with the Holy Spirit.

Ananias walks in the same pattern we have noted many times in this chapter. This ordinary Christian receives a vision, most likely in his daily devotional time, and gets the precise location where Saul, later known as the apostle Paul, is staying, and goes there. God uses him to lay hands on him and open Saul's blind eyes, which is a notable miracle, and prays for him to receive the baptism of the Holy Spirit. Paul would go on to plant churches, write a significant part of the New Testament, share the Gospel with Caesar, and move in powerful signs and wonders.

Ananias played a crucial part in all of this coming to fruition. It was no accident. If God used Ananias to bring cultural shift through his act of obedience, God could use you. Don't let a lack of degrees, natural abilities, speaking capabilities, or position deter you. There is such immeasurable power in prayer. Pray, watch God move in and through you, witness His miracle-working power, preach Jesus, and watch people give their lives to Christ. That's how cultural revolution and national awakening will start—through you!

IGNITING PRAYER

God, I ask you today to continue building my prayer life. I thank you that it's not out of a place of special abilities that the miraculous will flow, but out of a person's prayer life. I thank you that this truth qualifies me right where I am.

I confess to you today, Jesus, that I will pray, and I ask you to do your part, as you did after the apostles prayed in Acts 4. Stretch forth your hand and perform the miraculous. I ask you to heal the sick and raise the dead through my life. In your name, Amen.

I Will Possess a Heart for the Lost

The Power of Prayer and Evangelism Working Together

Prayer is pivotal in advancing the Church, as we noted in the previous chapter. Let's turn our attention now to a more modern example of prayer's powerful role when coupled with proclamation and evangelism. Charles Grandison Finney personifies what God can do with someone devoted to prayer and proclamation. Finney also shows the power of working intentionally with like-minded people, as we will note through his relationship with one of his colleagues, Father Daniel Nash.

The First Great Awakening that took place in the 1730s and '40s in the American colonies was long over, and staleness had set into the Church. By the turn of the century, Bible colleges were full of skeptics who would rationalize away all spirituality. Another awakening was needed.

God did send yet another earthshaking revival to awaken America again. Starting in the late 1780s and lasting until the 1840s, the Second Great Awakening began breaking forth.[1] Author and church historian Roberts Liardon asserts that this awakening lasted from the War of 1812 to the Civil War.[2] A revival in Cane Ridge, Kentucky, would begin the swell that would soon flood the United States. James McGready and Barton Stone were used powerfully in Kentucky, and would help pave the way for a historic move of God.

Charles Grandison Finney

One of the greatest evangelists to minister in the United States at this time was Charles G. Finney, a central figure in the Second Great Awakening. His ministry shook the nation and is credited with over five hundred thousand salvations. It's worth noting that this was before any modern advertising. The telephone still hadn't been invented, let alone the internet. Finney's methods for the altar call and his preaching style reshaped how ministers communicated in his day. Liardon comments in his series GOD'S GENERALS that Finney may have been the most innovative and anointed evangelist ever to walk the earth.[3]

The seventh child of a large family, Charles Grandison Finney was born in Warren, Connecticut, on August 29, 1792, to Sylvester and Rebecca Finney. The inspiration for his name came from Sir Charles Grandison, a character in a novel by an English aristocrat named Samuel Richardson. Though Sylvester Finney was presumably well-read, Charles stated in his later years that he never once heard his father pray, and the first time his father read the Bible was at the age of twenty-nine.

As a brilliant teenager, Charles Finney became a teacher at only fifteen or sixteen years old, and later became a schoolmaster. He was also a great athlete who stood six feet two inches tall. In his biography about Finney, Basil Miller quoted Finney's grandson as saying of him, "He excels every man and boy he met in every species of toil or sport. No man could throw him, knock his hat off, run faster, jump farther, leap higher, or throw a ball with as great force or precision."[4]

Finney later decided to join the navy and went to Sackets Harbor to enlist. Upon arrival, he found the area appalling and heard more foul language there than he had heard in his entire life. Young, attractive prostitutes in this town repulsed him rather than tempted him. His grandson describes an interaction Finney had with one of these women before he knew Christ: "He looked at her in wonder, and when he comprehended the nature of her request, he was so overcome with pity for her . . . that his cheeks burned, and before he could check it, he was shedding tears. . . . She, moved to shame, wept too."[5] Because of his strong moral compass, Finney returned to Connecticut, where he was born.

Eventually, Finney moved to a New Jersey town just outside New York City, where he first attended religious services. The services didn't impact him, however, as he felt they were dry. He considered attending Yale, but his parents persuaded him to study under Judge Benjamin Wright in Adams, New York. Although he never attended law school, he passionately prepared for and took on the profession of practicing law.

During this season of life, Finney began to attend prayer meetings once a week at a Presbyterian church. He noted in his autobiography that the meetings intrigued him, so he purchased a Bible for the first time.[6] After attending these meetings and reading the Bible, he concluded that he wasn't saved. The church pastor, George W. Gale, didn't believe Finney would ever get saved. This likely stemmed from Gale's Calvinistic viewpoint, which becomes very clear the more you read about him. Notably, Finney said before he was saved that he disagreed with the theology of predestination after reading the Bible for himself. He thought people blindly believed the preacher and instead needed to read the Bible for themselves. Imagine if Finney had succumbed to the doctrine of predestination and had not submitted to the call of the evangelist, thinking, *If people are predestined, why should I preach?* Imagine if Finney had not picked up a Bible and read it for himself. What a loss the entire Body of Christ would have felt if Finney had left his fate in the errant doctrine of this pastor. Yet there are examples of some Calvinists like George Whitefield and Charles Spurgeon who were powerful soul winners.

Observing the congregants' prayers, Finney wrote later that he noticed none of their requests were being answered. On one occasion, they asked him if they could pray for him. Their pastor, however, told them not to pray, because there was no hope for Finney. Once again, we see this pastor's Calvinistic doctrine resurface. Gale declined and said they had "prayed enough to drive the devil out of [the city of] Adams"[7] Thus, Finney didn't think their prayers would do him any good. This provoked him to study the Word, and after discovering Luke 11:9–10, he concluded that their ineffective prayers resulted from a lack of faith.

It must be noted that Charles Finney almost became an atheist because he couldn't understand why people's prayers were never answered. He seems to allude to the meetings he attended as being dry and cold. This was a turnoff to him. May this convict us and bring us resolve not to settle for a powerless, dead prayer meeting. We cannot twist or manipulate God. However, He does respond to hunger and desperation. We therefore must not be content with continual and regular prayer meetings that are void of God's presence and power.

Thankfully, Finney searched the Scriptures for himself to find out why their prayers were unanswered. Through that process, God moved on his heart, which solidified God's reality for him. Finney now faced the fact that the Gospel is true, but said he then had to make a choice: submit to Christ or deny Him.[8] Over several days, Finney grew anguished over his soul and embarrassed about his study of the Bible and prayer. He knew that if he died, he would go to hell. Liardon wrote that at this point, questions began to fill Finney's mind: "What are you waiting for? Did you not promise to give your heart to God? And what are you trying to do? Are you endeavoring to work out a righteousness of your own?"[9]

Finney finally concluded that he needed Jesus' finished work on the cross for salvation, not any of his own works of righteousness. He received the revelation of atonement. Then he heard, "Will you accept it today?" He replied, "Yes; I will accept it today or die in the attempt."[10]

What hunger and resolve from this man who was not yet saved. He would rather die than not break through to God. Finney decided to slip off into the woods to pray on his way to work. However, he was somewhat embarrassed that someone might see him, so he went further in. He then thought, *I must pray very quietly unless someone were to hear me.* His thoughts and actions convicted Finney, and he began to pray. While he was on his knees confessing his sins, God reminded him of a Scripture: "Then you will call upon me and come and pray to me, and I will hear you. You will seek me and find me, when you seek me with all your heart" (Jeremiah 29:12–13). Finney cried out with all his might and repented of his sins. Conviction of sin came, and all the guilt left his soul. This burden now lifted, Finney worried that he had somehow grieved the Holy Spirit. However, he declared that he would "preach the gospel if he converted."[11]

After his conversion, Finney returned to the law office and began worshiping. As the sun set, everyone left the office for the night, but Finney stayed behind. After the final person left, Finney closed the door, turned to pray, and felt Jesus walk into the room, later saying, "It seemed as if I met the Lord Jesus Christ face to face."[12] Finney describes the encounter as being in his mind, yet as if Jesus stood with him in the room "face to face."[13] He noted, "He said nothing but looked at me in such a manner as to break me right down at his feet."[14] While in this state for hours, Finney received the baptism in the Holy Spirit, who saturated his body and soul. The manifestation was so strong that he began to "bellow out the unutterable gushing of my heart."[15] Finney told God that he couldn't bear any more lest he die, yet he didn't fear death. The "unutterable gushings" were likely tongues; according to his autobiography, Finney believed tongues signified the baptism in the Holy Spirit.[16]

The next day, Finney determined to fulfill his vow to preach the Gospel. He went to the office, and one of his clients asked him about the case Finney was working on for him. To his surprise, Finney told him, "I have a retainer from the Lord Jesus Christ to plead His cause, and I cannot plead yours."[17] In disbelief, the man, a deacon at the Baptist church, questioned him: "What do you mean?"[18] Finney then explained what had happened to him the previous day and how he intended to preach the Gospel and give up practicing law. The deacon went home and began to pray because he had backslidden. Finney's word impacted him so much that he recommitted his life to the Lord.

This cannot be passed by. Finney didn't let any time pass and instantly stepped out in faith. This radical act pleased the Lord. Finney had no guarantee of income and no place to preach, yet he stepped out. We wonder why we don't see many like Charles Finney on the earth today, but how many are willing to pay the price and take the risk he took? May God grant us the grace so that when He says jump, we jump.

The late evangelist Reinhard Bonnke had the grace to jump. He once felt God speak to him about purchasing an office complex to host Christ for all Nations staff and ministry. Throughout the years, he hadn't felt they were supposed to do so. Yet God said to do it. So the following Saturday morning after he heard this, he drove to meet Daniel Kolenda, the new CEO of Christ for all Nations. Bonnke told him, "We must get a building."

Daniel replied, "What would you like me to do? It's a Saturday."

Bonnke replied, "I know you cannot do anything today. I wanted God to see a response from me because He is watching. When He speaks, I want Him to see me jump."[19]

God, may your Church respond in the same manner as these great men.

Two Staples of Spiritual Formation

We can see two staples in Charles Finney's spiritual formation before and after his salvation, staples he would carry throughout the rest of his life: devotion to prayer and study of the Word. Even before he was saved, he was drawn to prayer meetings. Finney's commitment to prayer throughout his life and ministry set the bar high and sustained his ministry. His prayer life paved the way for God to use him as the leading voice in the Second Great Awakening. His devotion to praying for revival and crying out for the lost remains unparalleled in the twenty-first century.

Further, when Finney thought about why the people in his church didn't receive answers to prayer, he also discovered other reasons: They did nothing to show that they had a burden for what they prayed over. They prayed for the lost to be saved, but never evangelized. They prayed *Thy Kingdom come*, but did nothing for it to come. Finney realized that their lives didn't align with receiving answers to prayer.[20] They prayed halfheartedly and didn't possess any fervency according to

James 5:16, "The effectual fervent prayer of a righteous man availeth much" (kjv).[21] Because of this realization, he sought fervently to live his life in alignment with his prayers.

Evangelist Reinhard Bonnke said, "You can get on your knees and pray twenty-four hours a day for God to save the lost. But no one will get saved until someone gets up and shares the Gospel."[22] He also said, "God works with workers, but he does not sit with sitters."[23] No one will argue the value and high importance prayer has. However, it must be coupled with a proclamation and stepping out. Both prayer and evangelism are vitally important. When connected, as the apostles displayed above, the combination will once again shake the world.

The second discipline that formed Finney spiritually consisted of his study of the Word. He didn't take the religious leaders of the day or his pastor at their word. He studied the Bible for himself and followed it to the utmost of his ability. Finney's study of Scripture led him to form different theological perspectives, so Pastor Gale and many other pastors felt his theology was off concerning Calvinism. Finney disagreed with Gale's theology of limited atonement. Finney argued that God made atonement available to all, and that one must accept it and repent to receive salvation.[24]

In an excerpt from one of Finney's later sermons, he clearly states that "God intended to impress on all minds these two great truths: first, that man is ruined by his sin; second, that he may be saved through Jesus Christ."[25] Though some encouraged him to attend Princeton, he believed preachers who studied there were boring and unable to connect with the people.[26] He also felt strongly that people needed to read the Bible for themselves rather than rely on their pastors' word. Thus, the study of the Word and prayer remained of primary importance to Finney, and they greatly impacted his spiritual formation.

Inspired Preaching

Finney didn't pursue degrees, yet the Lord leads many to do so, including me. However, the core of his burden was his desire to walk in the anointing of the Holy Spirit above anything and everything—not the inventions of man to draw a crowd, but the presence of God to attract the masses. What a novel idea. Finney not only showed us it's possible, but he also showed us how. He took notes from the early apostles and again married prayer and evangelism. He didn't use notes for the first ten years of his ministry, but preached by inspiration and divine unction, which was made possible due to his robust prayer life.[27]

For example, in one meeting, when Finney was finishing a sermon, a man approached and pleaded with him to come to his village and preach. He agreed to the request and arrived the next day at a packed school that had never held a religious gathering. Finney promptly got on his knees to pray. Not knowing what he would speak, he prayed until he felt a release, which was after about an hour, and spontaneously shared a seemingly random verse: "Up, get you out of this place; for the LORD will destroy this city" (Genesis 19:14 KJV).[28] Remember that these were all unchurched, lost people he was in the midst of. Yet he got on his knees and prayed for an hour. No music, no PowerPoint, no one talking—just Finney on his knees, praying. Many today would say you could never do this. I would say it's better to preach with unction than to share and articulate a written sermon without it.

In this school, he explained how Abraham prayed and spoke with God about saving the righteous from the city because of his nephew Lot. As he spoke, Finney noticed the crowd becoming angry in such a manner that he thought violence would soon follow. He didn't understand why his words seemed to cause such a rage. After speaking to the people for nearly fifteen minutes and pressing for their souls, he stopped talking. The meeting grew solemn and quiet for two minutes, and then people suddenly began falling out of their chairs and crying out to God. The noise grew so loud that Finney could no longer preach. No one could hear him as he told the people, "You're not in hell yet; now let me direct you to Christ."[29]

Finney then walked over to a young man and spoke in his ear to share the Gospel. As soon as he received the words, the man calmed down for about two minutes and started crying again and praying for others. This lasted hours in the same fashion as Finney talked with people one by one. Eventually, he had to leave to preach at another location, but the service continued without him until the following day. When Finney came back to the town, he discovered why the people had initially grown so angry. The nickname for the town was Sodom, and the man who had invited him was Lot! The people thought Finney knew the story, but he did not. God showed up in power and vindicated him.

Early and often, we see the combination of prayer and proclamation that brings tremendous harvest. Finney's preaching was prophetic and had profound results. It would do everyone who preaches and teaches good to preach out of divine unction and not just intellect and well-crafted sermons. The difference between a good sermon and a great sermon is the anointing of the Holy Spirit. Crafty points, savvy transitions, a big idea, intellectual prowess, or charisma don't make a great sermon. God's presence filling the room makes a sermon great, and that comes from no other means outside prayer. Addictions are not broken by good humor and a likable communicator. They are broken by the anointing. You can be humorous and charismatic while also carrying a strong anointing. Above all is the anointing that comes from the place of prayer. Finney displayed it here as his prayer life gave birth to anointed prophetic preaching.

The Revival Intensifies

One of Finney's first revivals took place in Evans Mills, New York.[30] After his first meeting there, he declared that they had chosen the devil when not responding to Christ in his sermon. In response, the second night was unbelievably packed. In the crowd was a woman married to a bar owner. At the meeting, God struck her dumb, leaving her slumped over and unconscious for sixteen hours. When she regained consciousness and her ability to speak, she confessed that she wasn't saved and gave her life to Christ.

In today's culture, many shrink back from strong statements that people have chosen the devil. In no way, shape, or form should we use that language to be provocative; on the other hand, we shouldn't water it down if we feel God is saying it. Many would say it would offend someone. Yet the next night, Finney's meeting was packed. He had obeyed God, and God gave the increase. Finney seemed to put a very high value on obedience, far above fearing what people might or might not think.

In Evans Mills, Finney became reacquainted with Father Daniel Nash. He had first met Nash during his license interview and felt that Nash was in a backslidden state.[31] (Finney was being licensed; Nash was a presbyter.) Shortly after their first interaction, Nash contracted a terrible eye disease that caused him to stay in a dark room for several weeks.[32] During this time, he did nothing but pray and came out transformed. Nash had used a prayer strategy of writing the names of the lost on a piece of paper and praying for them several times a day. He also maintained a list he called the "hard case list," which included a bar owner in the city who opposed the revival and was abusive toward Christians. After Nash's prayers for him, the man attended one of Finney's meetings. During the service, conviction fell upon him so much that he stood up and cried aloud, repenting of his sins. This bar owner subsequently turned his bar into a prayer chapel throughout the rest of Finney's ministry there.

My wife and I use the same prayer strategy as Nash personally and as a tool to train churches in praying for the lost. We give out bookmarks where individuals can write the names of five people down on five different lines. At the bottom, there's another place to write the same names and then tear them off and give them to the church, where the leadership can pray over them. My wife and I have seen God move in powerful ways through this strategy.

During this visit to Evans Mills, Nash and Finney began to work together as a team. Nash went into a town three or four weeks before Finney arrived and prayed in twelve-hour shifts with another prophetic intercessor named Abel Clary. The burden of God was so heavy upon Nash that he couldn't leave his room due to the agony he felt in prayer, with loud travailing for the lost. While in Gouverneur, New York, Finney preached while Brother Nash prayed without ceasing.[33] Some young people came to oppose the revival, prompting Nash to stand up and say, "Now, mark me, young men! God will break your ranks in less than a week, either by converting some of you or sending others to hell. He will do this as certainly as the Lord is my God!"[34] On Tuesday of the same week, the leader of the young men came to Finney, broken over his sin, and repented, and all the young men were saved. I wouldn't encourage anyone to go try this approach. Father Nash had learned to hear God over a long period of time. If you are confident God gives you a word like this, step out, but be aware that missing it concerning such a word could hurt people rather than help them.

In New York Mills, Minnesota, locals invited Finney to tour the town's factory.[35] As he walked into the building, he noticed a young lady having trouble with her work. She trembled as she tried to sew. When Finney came within ten feet of her station, she suddenly sank in the chair and began sobbing loudly in deep conviction of sin. In a matter of moments, workers throughout the room began weeping because of the presence of God. Finney describes the moment as a powder keg exploding. The whole factory came under the conviction of the Holy Spirit. The owner temporarily shut down operations so people could give themselves fully over to God. This lasted a couple of days, and by the end of the revival, nearly everyone was gloriously saved. Three thousand people were saved during the revival in New York Mills, and after eight months every one of the three thousand still attended church.

What a remarkable move of God. Be sure that these kinds of outbreaks aren't meant to be confined to history. God wants and desires to do the same thing again in this generation. We must therefore dedicate ourselves to prayer and obedience, like Nash and Finney. Their lives were laid down sacrificially through prayer and proclamation. Ask God what He wants you to do. It will incorporate prayer and proclamation, but possibly in a different method.

Whatever the method, I believe the mantle of Finney and Nash is on the ground, waiting for someone to pick it up. How about you? Why not now? It isn't prideful or arrogant to ask God to use you like Finney and Nash. Ask Him to pick you right now. Put down this book and cry out to God, *Pick me! Pick me!* Where are the Finneys and Nashes of this generation? This generation needs such catalysts. Ask God to use you, as He did them!

Finney's Later Years

After years of heavy travel and doctors encouraging him to take a break, Finney took a position as pastor in April 1832 at Second Free Presbyterian Church. However, he never stopped traveling and holding revivals. The revivals led to God calling countless individuals into ministry, and the young ministers needed to train someplace where they wouldn't be indoctrinated with Calvinism. As a result, Finney took a position at Oberlin College to teach theology, and subsequently became president of the school in 1851.[36]

Finney continued to travel and spark revivals everywhere he preached. His approach had a proven track record. As he said himself in his memoirs, "The measures were simply preaching the gospel, and abundant prayer, in private, in social circles, and public prayer meetings; much stress being always laid upon prayer as an essential means of promoting the revival."[37]

Notably, one of Finney's most challenging setbacks in life resulted from losing the love of his life and mother of their six children, Lydia Finney.[38] She had prayed for Charles's conversion, and had given him faithful support that surely wasn't easy due to his heavy travel schedule. However, she was also known as a reformer and joined him on many revival tours across the country, leading women's prayer sessions.[39] She suffered with illness for many years and eventually died at the age of 43 on December 17, 1847. Almost five years later, tragedy struck again when Finney's youngest child, Delia, died.

Finney married a second time, but his marriage to Elizabeth Ford Atkinson seemed to be more for convenience since he still had small children at home. After she died, he married a third time; his new wife was Rebecca Allen Rayl. From 1851 to 1857, Finney continued traveling and holding powerful revivals throughout the Northeast and overseas, in England and Scotland. His last trip to England, however, taxed him tremendously, so when he arrived back to Oberlin in 1860, he didn't leave again. Finney taught and spoke at Oberlin the rest of his life, but resigned as president in 1866. Charles Granderson Finney's final day on this earth was August 16, 1875.

Second to None

God clearly used Finney through his many revivals to bring about the Second Great Awakening. However, this would not have happened had Finney not laid a strong spiritual foundation through those two staples of a fervent prayer life and study of the Word. His prayer life was the breeding ground for all God did through his life and ministry. Few have accomplished what Finney and Father Nash did as they interceded for revival and the salvation of souls.

Finney remained committed to intentional quality time with God and had no use for mindless repetition in prayer. He firmly believed prayer should engage one's entire mind, soul, and body.[40] This directly contrasted with the way the Pharisees prayed, using their many words while their hearts were far from God. Finney also believed that the desires of a person's heart need sanctification in order for the person to pray in a way that would affect the Kingdom of God, as taught in the Lord's Prayer. He stated explicitly,

> A desire that God's Kingdom should be set up in the world and all men become holy. The will is set upon this as the highest and most to be desired of all objects, whatever. It becomes the supreme desire of the soul, and all other things sink into comparative insignificance before it.[41]

In other words, believers should wholly desire God's Kingdom on earth, and their prayer life should reflect that.

Charles G. Finney gave his life to the work of the Lord in a manner second to none. His devotion to prayer that brings revival, and to the sacrifice of his entire life to study and preach the Gospel, remain remarkable, as illustrated by his own words: "There are two kinds of means requisite to promote a revival: one to influence men, the other to influence God. The truth is employed to influence men, and prayer to move God."[42] Finney's example has much to teach the Church today. If we pray in a manner of total devotion and give our selves in abandonment to the uncompromised preaching of the Gospel that entails a holy life, the United States and the West will see a Third Great Awakening.

Finney and Nash embodied the theme of this book. Their prayer ignited revival. They lived it out. It's now time for another generation who will not take no for an answer to pound the doors of heaven until they open once again and the Spirit is poured out in an unprecedented manner.

Revival often comes in a plethora of different styles and manifestations. As we have seen, Charles Finney's contribution to the Second Great Awakening mainly came through his itinerant ministry as he traveled from city to city. It wasn't normative for him to stay in one area for months. He would often move from place to place without putting down deep roots in any one city. God has used many evangelists in this manner. Yet this isn't the only way God uses people. You don't have to be an evangelist to be used in revival and awakening!

In our next chapter, we will look at William J. Seymour's life and how God used him to birth revival. He was much different from Finney in a variety of ways. Seymour had a very different upbringing and style of ministry. It's refreshing that God uses a variety of individuals and doesn't require everyone to be the same. May you and I be catalysts for the next revival and forerunners for the next Great Awakening!

IGNITING PRAYER

God, I thank you for Charles Finney and Daniel Nash. However, they are now with you. God, where are the Finneys of my time? Where are the Nashes? I don't see any men like these giants of the faith.

Lord, since I don't see any, raise me up. Pick me, use me, anoint me, put your Spirit upon me! May I continually increase my devotion to your Word and to prayer, as Finney was devoted to them. May my spiritual life affect not only my own spiritual growth, but the people around me by making me a catalyst for revival in our time. In the name of Jesus, Amen!

I Will Not Focus on My Limitations

The Power of Humility and Faithfulness

Throughout the span of time, God has used individuals who wouldn't be at the top of the list, based on their mere human wisdom and understanding. Samuel would never have picked David to become king, for example. His eyes were on cultural norms and outward appearance. Thank the Lord that His standard isn't based on looks, experience, economic prowess, education, or gifts as prerequisites. God looks at the heart.

The religious people of the day wouldn't have picked Peter and John as God's men, either. These men were depicted as unschooled and ordinary. They hadn't attended higher education or learned from those deemed the experts in order to be qualified for ministry. Not to mention the examples of Esther, Moses, Gideon, or Mary and Joseph, for that matter. Esther was an orphan raised by her cousin who happened to be a royal official (see Esther 2:7). Gideon hid himself from the enemy, and on self-examination concluded that he was totally inadequate. Yet an angel of the Lord appeared and said, "The LORD is with you, mighty warrior" (Judges 6:12 NIV). Those called by God all throughout the Old Testament regularly claimed their inadequacy. It's common that the weak become strong, the least become great, the mean become mighty, and the last become first.[1]

Some would argue that William J. Seymour is the father of modern Pentecost, or at least the catalyst God used as the embryonic seed to birth many Pentecostal movements in America and worldwide. Observing what Seymour endured and where he came from will encourage you greatly that God can do the same for you. America looked very different during the timeframe of his birth and the start of his ministry than it does today. Looking at Seymour's context will give us a great appreciation for him and also faith in what God can and will do in and through us.

Seymour didn't allow lack, racism, poverty, segregation, misunderstandings, rejection, and many other setbacks to deter him from believing in God and being used mightily. He never made excuses. He never blamed anyone or played the victim card. Yet if anyone ever had such a card, it was Seymour. Let's look at why this is so profound.

Against a Stacked Deck

William J. Seymour was born in Centerville, Louisiana, on May 2, 1870.[2] His parents were former slaves who were both the children of slaves. His father, Simon, could neither read nor write because most slave owners prohibited their slaves from learning. Seymour's birth was only five short years after the Civil War ended.[3] During the time of his birth, the economic engine of this region was driven by cotton, sugarcane, rice, and cattle. Prior to the Civil War, St. Mary Parish had one of the most flourishing plantations in the state. It was sadly due to slavery that Louisiana and this particular parish were strong economically.

In Louisiana, two out of every five families owned slaves. This equates to roughly 40 percent of white families enslaving people. That's almost half the white population. The state itself also owned slaves. This led to a whopping 47 percent of the entire state being enslaved. In Seymour's city, four hundred people owned close to thirteen thousand enslaved people.

Laws toward slaves were inhumane and barbaric. The law allowed a black person to be executed for hitting a white person even in a way that caused only a mere bruise. If a black person hit a white person three consecutive times, it was considered cause for death. If any enslaved person fled, didn't stop on command, and was shot, the law protected the white person as having just cause. The slave could die and there would be no charges filed. This shows no regard for life. The attitude of the South toward slaves can be summarized in one statement from a South Carolina chancellor of the Court of Appeals: "A free African population is a curse to any country."[4] What a sad moment in America.

The aftermath of the war caused economic hardship. Farms that had been worth $248 million in 1860 were only worth $110 million after the war. Farm equipment that had been worth $18 million before the war was only worth $7 million by 1890. This didn't bode well for freed slaves. The angst and anger that would be funneled in their direction through segregation and flat-out racism would be horrific. For example, the Jim Crow laws were state and local laws introduced in the Southern United States in the late nineteenth and early twentieth centuries that enforced racial segregation, and *Jim Crow* was a derogative term for an African American.[5] Far from promoting equality, as a body of law, Jim Crow institutionalized economic, educational, political, and social disadvantages and second class citizenship for most African Americans living in the United States.[6]

After Seymour's mother and father were freed from slavery, they continued to work on the plantation. As Seymour got older, he worked on a plantation as well. The lack of education didn't cause Seymour to give up on learning. He taught himself to read through reading the Bible.[7]

You'd think the Church of the time would have served as a refuge for African Americans, but that wasn't the case. One denominational publication stated in 1874, "There is but one way now to manage the Negro. He is, as a class, amenable to neither reason nor gratitude. He must be starved into the common perceptions of decency."[8] What a horrific and unjust statement.

Seymour would have endured poverty and racism throughout his childhood. The deck was stacked against him. How could this man be used in any great manner with America so racially divided? How could he gain any footing with all the persecution due to his skin color? He was disenfranchised and poor. The education for African Americans was minuscule at best. Seymour was born the same year as Virginia law made it illegal for black and white children to attend the same schools.[9] When he was twelve, 49 Black people were lynched; when he was twenty-two, 161 more were lynched.[10]

Southern Democrats actively wrote Jim Crow laws and instituted customs that oppressed African Americans, legalized discrimination against them, and prevented them from access to voting. Jim Crow laws touched every part of life, so black and white workers couldn't be in the same room, enter the same door, or gaze out the same window.[11] Many industries wouldn't hire Black people, and unions passed rules to exclude them. Even in 1914, long after the Azusa Street Revival, some states forbade Black people to leave their homes after 10 p.m. and had signs marked "whites only" for doors, ticket windows, drinking fountains, etc. Prisons, hospitals, and orphanages were segregated. There were also unwritten rules barring Black people from certain jobs and stores. So many unjust laws in society made it seemingly impossible at this time in American history for Seymour to be used by God in any manner that would have a profound impact, let alone involve integrated services or have any global reach.

Changing the Trajectory

Willian Seymour left Louisiana and headed North, but it's a myth to say that life was considerably better up North.[12] He moved to Indianapolis. While there, he was converted. He joined an all-Black church called Simpson Chapel Methodist Episcopal Church. Seymour's life would no longer be the same; he was made new as his old self died and was resurrected in Christ. His salvation would change the trajectory of his entire life.

Seymour then moved to Chicago, although he wouldn't live there for an extended time. It's very likely and presumed that during his time in Chicago, he encountered the ministry of John Alexander Dowie. Dowie was known for the mighty miracles taking place through his ministry. One of the reasons it's thought that Seymour would have been in his meetings is due to Dowie's stance on segregation.[13] He believed in integration and would have white and Black people sitting together. On his board of twelve apostles, he also reserved one committed place to be filled by an African American. He was way ahead of his time for this kind of reconciliation. This could be where the seeds for the supernatural were profoundly planted in Seymour.

Seymour later moved to Houston, Texas, where he would step in and serve as pastor for Lucy Farrow, who was on her way to work for Charles F. Parham. When Farrow returned to Houston from her time in Kansas, she told Seymour how she had been baptized in the Holy Spirit, with the evidence of speaking in tongues. Later, Charles Parham would also relocate to Houston, Texas. Seymour attended the services there, and his hunger for God and the baptism in the Holy Spirit continued to grow. He then enrolled in Parham's Bible school. During this time, Seymour gave himself to fasting and prayer. He understood the season he was in while training for ministry and didn't waste time. We cannot overvalue his devotion while in Houston. He took full advantage of every moment he had and seized his opportunity to press in. Let's let his example encourage us to redeem the time, as he did. Press in and go after God!

While attending Bible school, Seymour faced racism and segregation in a place that should not have stood for such injustice. He wasn't allowed to sit with the white students. He wasn't even allowed to tarry at the altar with them. This was believed to have inhibited him from receiving the baptism of the Holy Spirit at that time.[14] White people would have had the opportunity to tarry, but not Seymour. However, this didn't inhibit him from excelling in his studies.

Seymour didn't allow these injustices to cause him to walk in unforgiveness and offense. If he had held offense and allowed bitterness to set in, it would have affected the call of God on his life. Many are offended by far less persecution than Seymour had to endure. Many get bitter over things possibly quite minuscule. This is one of the enemy's favorite tools. May we all take notes from Seymour. No one would have judged him for holding a grudge against Parham and leaving the school. In direct contrast, he loved and respected Parham. There were no hard feelings, and Seymour even invited Parham to speak for him years later. In Seymour's preaching, we never find racially charged sermons blaming white people for the atrocities. He walked in forgiveness. Azusa gives us a blueprint for reconciliation: *forgiveness*. Through forgiveness, God used Seymour in a miraculous manner that would bring the races together. This shows us a path forward for us today: *forgiveness*.

The Early Onset of Revival

A woman named Neely Terry visited Houston from the West Coast and visited Seymour's church. While there, she received the baptism of the Holy Spirit. After Neely returned to California, she invited him to come share the apostolic faith message with her church. He felt the leading of the Lord in this and headed to California. Parham didn't feel it was God that wanted Seymour to leave, but since Seymour persisted, an offering was taken to help him get there. It must be noted that even though California wasn't what the Deep South was regarding segregation, it still wasn't free of racism.

At the time of William Seymour's arrival in California, Los Angeles was in a season of deep spiritual hunger, with many leaders and churches desperate for revival. When revival broke, it was no accident. Many, many were contending for a move of God. Many of the churches were praying specifically for a return of first-century Pentecost.

One of the evangelists in the city was Frank Bartleman, who carried a deep spirit of prayer. For fifteen months before revival finally broke, he was in solitude and prayer, carrying a tremendous burden. He stated, "Day and night the Spirit was heavy upon me . . . until it seemed I must die."[15] His wife felt that the weighty burden on him might take his life. The neighbors thought he was very ill due to the groans they would continually hear coming from his room. Bartleman said, "The groanings that cannot be uttered had seized me. I was in birth pangs. At night I would roll and groan in my sleep. And [my] wife declared I was pleading for souls even then. The mighty divine compassion, travail, and agony for souls had gripped me, and I could not shake it off."[16]

Revival is never an accident. Azusa Street didn't come about in one day; a plethora of intercessors like Bartleman birthed it. Los Angeles was entering a season of divine hunger for saints and leaders who were desperate for God.

Another leader in L.A. named Joseph Smale, who pastored First Baptist Church, caught a burden for revival while on sabbatical. During his time away he traveled overseas, and one of his many stops was Wales. This was during the great Welsh Revival. While there, he built a friendship with Evan Roberts, the revival leader. Upon returning to the States, he felt First Baptist should lead L.A. into a revival, which would be birthed through prayer. He preached about his experience in the Welsh Revival, and that particular service lasted over three hours.[17] Divine hunger was brewing in this Baptist congregation, and the church held extended revival services for fifteen weeks, meeting twice daily at 2:15 p.m. and 7:45 p.m. They believed for revival. Again, we see the forerunners of divine hunger and prayer converging.

A religious spirit rose in the church, however, and they pushed Pastor Smale to resign. His board came against him, demanding that things return to the way they were before his trip to Wales. He decided to leave due to the board's lack of vision for revival. The clerk closed one meeting's board minutes by stating, "May God have mercy on this church for rejecting His anointed."[18]

Bartleman also attended this revival and was grieved, stating, "What an awful position for a church to take, to throw God out."[19]

Smale started a new church, and 190 members followed him. He named his new church First New Testament Church. Their fervent cry for revival continued. Pastor Elmer K. Fisher, who led a Baptist church in Glendale, California, was also hungry for revival. He often went to his church and prayed through the night for revival. As he preached and pressed in for a move of God, his church rejected him as well and asked him to resign. He then joined Smale at New Testament Church.

You can see that revival will cost you. It cost these men their jobs and reputations. They wanted to have revival rather than be part of churches that didn't have a spiritual appetite for the things of God.

Another leader and evangelist, F. B. Meyer, was also preaching and stirring people up for revival in the area. We see here a convergence of the hungry. Hunger and prayer are the prerequisites for any move of God, and these were evident in not just a few believers in that area, but in many.

Frank Bartleman's hunger and pursuit of God continued as he earnestly prayed for revival. He wrote evangelist Evan Roberts, leader of the Welsh Revival.[20] His letter requested prayer for those in California. In a letter Roberts wrote back to Bartleman, he stated, "I am impressed by your sincerity and honesty of purpose. Congregate the people who are willing to make a total surrender. Pray and wait. Believe God's promises. Hold daily meetings. May God bless you, is my earnest prayer."[21]

Methodist churches throughout L.A. were also hungry and seeking God for revival. In March 1906, First Methodist Church held ten straight days of meetings where they sought and believed God for revival.

Mrs. Julia Hutchins [22]and eight families were kicked out of Second Baptist Church during this time. Hutchins's teachings deviated from strict Baptist doctrine and wouldn't be tolerated. These families began to attend Household of Faith near Bonnie Brae Street. They soon left there on the lines of segregation and color. They pitched a tent to meet in, but they would soon move to 214 Bonnie Brae Street, home of Richard and Ruth Asherry. They moved because winter was about to set in, and they knew the rains would have a negative effect on their tent meetings.

Crowds began to swell at 214 Bonnie Brae Street. Julia Hutchins led the meetings, but wrong doctrine crept in and others tried to gain control, so they needed a leader. Neely Terry, a cousin of the Asberrys, had recently returned from Houston, where she had received the baptism of the Holy Spirit. She recommended the godly man she had met while in Houston, none other than William J. Seymour. After much prayer, they gave him the invitation to come, along with the train fare he needed. He agreed to come deliver some Bible teachings. They believed he had already been baptized in the Holy Spirit and didn't know that he, too, was seeking the baptism.

These humble saints had been praying for over a year to have more power with God for the salvation of lost and suffering humanity. Here we observe what seems to have been their chief activity—none other than prayer. These individuals carried a deep burden for revival and cried out continually for the Lord to come in a demonstration of power through a fresh outpouring of the Holy Spirit. As I have noted, not just those gathered at Bonnie Brae Street, but many leaders, churches, and ministries were crying out to God for the same outpouring of the Holy Spirit. God stirred His Church in Los Angeles, California, and His Church responded in prayer, supplication, and divine hunger. Will prayer and hunger again be the forerunners to revival in our time?

The Initial Outpouring

Before William Seymour arrived to hold services, the meetings were moved from Bonnie Brae Street to a larger building due to the increase of people attending. A small building on

9th and Santa Fe was rented out to hold the services. The people were eager to meet Seymour, and he arrived on February 22, 1906. One of the many topics he began to minister on was the baptism of the Holy Spirit and speaking in tongues. However, Seymour still had not yet experienced the baptism for himself.

Seymour one day asked the people to meet him back at the church at 3:00 to pray and seek God for the baptism. Pastor Julia Hutchins didn't agree with Seymour's theology on tongues and locked him and his supporters out of the building. Now Seymour found himself hundreds of miles from home without a place to preach, and with a seemingly impossible path forward to fulfill his mission. He also found himself with little to no money. Edward S. Lee from the Peniel Mission invited him to his house for lunch. When Lee heard what Seymour was going through, he didn't send him back out on the streets. Despite reservations, Lee allowed him to stay in his home.

Seymour stayed in his room in Lee's house and gave himself over to fasting and prayer. Long before his burden for Pentecost, he had a deep hunger for more of God. John G. Lake, who was a personal friend of Seymour, recalls him saying,

> Brother, before I met Parham, such a hunger to have more of God was in my heart that I prayer for five hours a day for two and a half years. I got to Los Angeles, and when I got there the hunger was not less but more. I prayed, God, what can I do? And the Spirit said, pray more. But Lord, I am praying five hours a day now. I increased my hours of prayer to seven, and prayed on for a year and a half more. I prayed God give me what Parham preached, the real Holy Ghost and fire with tongues and love and power of God like the apostles had.[23]

Lee and Seymour began to pray and seek God together every day for the baptism of the Holy Spirit. Other men from the church would join them. Some would pray the entire night, while others would leave their jobs to pray and contend for revival. Lee was now overcome with a spirit of prayer. Even while at work, he would hide away in the basement for hours to pray and seek God. He couldn't help himself. In one of these intense times of prayer, he had a vision of Peter and John coming toward him with their hands lifted up in the air, praying and shaking under the power of God, while both spoke in tongues. The Holy Spirit fell upon Lee, and he, too, began to shake under the power of God. He shared this experience with Seymour.

Lee's hunger for God intensified. One night as Lee's faith was high, he asked Seymour to lay hands upon him to receive the baptism. Seymour felt the time was right and laid his hands upon him in the name of Jesus. When he did, Lee fell to the floor. Mrs. Lee was stunned, began to cry, and asked what Seymour had done with her husband. With all the commotion and fear, Seymour felt that the Lord wouldn't finish the work at that time and asked Lee to get up. Lee had experienced such a touch from God, however, that he was never the same. After this encounter, he began to seek God day and night.

The meetings were soon moved back to 214 Bonnie Brae Street, and prayer was continuous. A few white visitors would come, including Frank Bartleman, who attended for the first time on March 26. The believers were intent on revival and sought God intensely for the next several weeks.

On April 6, services lasted long into the night, and Seymour encouraged everyone to begin a ten-day fast. The next two days, powerful services took place on Bonnie Brae. On the third day, Lee asked Seymour to again pray for him to receive the Holy Spirit. When Seymour laid hands on him, he was baptized in the Holy Spirit and began to speak in tongues.

That evening, the meeting started with a song, prayer, and some testimonies. At this particular time, only African

Americans were present. Seymour preached on the Holy Spirit, and his text was Acts 2:4. After the message, Lee lifted his hands and began to pray in the Spirit. Jennie Moore was on the organ stool and suddenly fell to the floor and began praying in tongues. She was the first woman in their congregation to receive the baptism.

When Moore hit the floor, many others fell as if they had all been struck by lightning. Some were in trances for five hours. At this point, many ran into the front yard while speaking in tongues and praising the Lord. Bud Traynor, just baptized in the Holy Spirit, was preaching and prophesying on the front porch. Jennie Moore prophesied in Hebrew. The meeting lasted until 10:00 p.m. this particular night. A Pentecostal revival had come to Bonnie Brae and would soon invade California and the entire world.

The next day, there was such a crowd that visitors couldn't get near the house.[24] Many persisted in their efforts to enter, and they were hit by the power of God and fell to the floor as they crossed the threshold of 214 Bonnie Brae. During the next three days, crowds of both Black and white people filled the yard, streets, and house. The scene was described this way: "The porch became the pulpit, and the street became the pews."[25] In just a few days, hundreds were saved, with many healed and baptized in the Holy Spirit. Mrs. G. V. Evans became the first white person to receive the baptism.[26] Eyewitnesses testified that the house shook in the same way as the disciples experienced in the Acts of the Apostles.

A notable healing took place at this early onset of revival, described this way by Emma Cotton,[27] an African American preacher and friend of Seymour who attended Azuza:

The noise of the great outpouring of the Spirit drew me. I had been nothing but a "walking drug store" all my life, with weak lungs and cancer. As they looked at me they said, "Child, God will heal you." In those days of the great outpouring, when they said God will heal you, you were healed. For thirty-three years, I have never gone back to the doctors, thank God, nor any of that old medicine! The Lord saved me, baptized me with the Holy Ghost, healed me, and sent me on my way rejoicing.[28]

Three days after the initial outpouring, on April 12, Seymour was seeking the baptism in the Holy Spirit.[29] He was praying with a white brother who was tired and felt the Lord wouldn't do it at that time. However, Seymour replied, "I am not going to give up."[30] In a short time, he was filled and began to speak in tongues. He said it was like a "sphere of fiery, white-hot radiance falling upon him."[31] The Asberrys' son said he "fell under the power of the Holy Ghost like he was dead and spoke in unknown tongues."[32] Seymour would later describe it this way: "We had prayed all night when at four o'clock in the morning, God came through the window."[33]

The windows of heaven were opened! God was answering the earnest prayer of the saints of Los Angeles. The early onset of revival had turned into an initial outpouring upon the seekers at Bonnie Brae. Salvations were taking place. More and more were baptized in the Holy Spirit. Healings were breaking out. Manifestations of the Spirit were normal as people were falling to the floor as dead under the power of the Lord. Many would shake under the power of the Spirit. God was meeting with His people. The Spirit of the Lord was upon them!

Moving to Azusa Street

As the crowds continued to swell, 214 Bonnie Brae could not accommodate the budding revival. An abandoned church building was discovered at 312 Azusa Street. This place would prove itself a humble beginning for God's actions. The flooring was just dirt on the ground. It had once been a horse stable, and there was visible fire damage on the walls, and no indoor plumbing. The only restroom was outside, behind the building.

Getting this building ready for services was a lot of work. The people covered the floor with sawdust and used straw for matting around the altar. They made a pulpit out of two shoe crates stacked on top of one another and covered with a cotton cloth. Nail kegs with wooden planks were brought in for seating, along with mismatched chairs. A Roman Catholic priest built and provided an altar.

There was a second floor in the building with an apartment that served as a home for Seymour. There was also a long upstairs room that stretched out the length of the building and was called the Pentecostal Upper Room.

Clara Lum, one individual very connected to Azusa, said, "It was the most humble place I was ever in for a meeting."[34] Many visitors compared the building to Bethlehem's manger. One of the members of First Methodist Church noted that they had been earnestly praying for revival to come to Los Angeles and were hoping it would start in their church.[35] However, they were thankful that it didn't start in any church and its beginning was in a barn. If it had started in a church, African Americans and Hispanics wouldn't have been able to attend. God wanted to pour out His Spirit on all flesh, not just one ethnicity.

Eminent Harvard professor of religion Dr. Harvey Cox commented on this in his book *Fire from Heaven,*

> Like the story of the ancient Israelites and the life of Jesus of Nazareth, it [the modern Pentecostal Movement] is another example of the way God uses unlikely vessels . . . to accomplish the divine purpose. Pouring the new blessing on a one-eyed black preacher and a gaggle of social outcasts is like choosing

a nation of slaves and the son of an unwed mother to begin new chapters of history.[36]

Jesus is very comfortable appearing in and making Himself known in humble and simple places, just like Azusa. Looking briefly at the beginning of Jesus' life on earth, we can observe some commonalities regarding Azusa and its humble beginning: "And she gave birth to her firstborn son and wrapped him in swaddling cloths and laid him in a manger, because there was no place for them in the inn" (Luke 2:7) This was a simple birth with no adornment, an extremely humble beginning. The newborn Jesus was placed in a feeding structure for animals. Mary laid him in the trough after she wrapped him.[37] Over the years, through many songs with lyrics such as "away in a manager," we are lured into picturing a nice, quaint atmosphere. Nothing could have been further from the truth, however. As one commentator on Luke wrote, "No one sings, 'Away in a feeding trough.'"[38] Luke is showing the audience that there was no lure of dignity in this humble place. No one would even give up his room for this pregnant mother so she could have a respectable birth. Rather, she and her husband were humiliated. Baby Jesus' head was first laid down where animals feed. Not only was He born where animals feed, but imagine the other conditions accompanying this situation—from bugs and rodents to the presence of animals, to animal wastes, to the smells, to name a few. The King of king's entrance was made in robust humility.

Humility is part of the nature of God. It was the first attribute we would observe in Jesus' life. It is one of the main attributes of Azusa in its beginning and through the duration of the revival. Looking at success in the West, big Hollywood-style productions are what many esteem. Yet Jesus and the Holy Spirit are often found in places that are minuscule and unattractive to modern societies. It would do the West well to look toward humility and simplicity because that's where God seems to be found, as it was at the very beginning of Jesus' life, and at the birth of Azusa.

Only a few months into the revival, up to thirteen hundred would attend, with eight hundred in the building and the rest outside on the boardwalk or close to the low windows, looking in. Seasoned ministers began to attend and were in awe of the power and majesty of God.[39] They would express that it was unlike anything that they had ever seen or felt.[40]

One of those seasoned ministers was William H. Durham. He was a very successful evangelist who ministered in nearly every large city in America.[41] The Lord used him in powerful ways, and Durham experienced deep personal encounters with the Holy Spirit. Yet when he arrived at Azusa, he encountered God in a manner he never had before. In one of the encounters, he felt electricity go through his body and became limp all over, and he lay under the power of God for two hours. On the night he was baptized in the Holy Spirit, he jerked and quaked for three hours. Describing this encounter, he shared how the Holy Spirit touched his whole body, section by section.[42] After being under the power for three hours, he was then baptized in the Holy Spirit and spoke in tongues. Seasoned ministers were being transformed in a profound manner. Azusa was intensifying.

Miraculous Meetings and Manifestations

The Azusa Street services were powerful and dynamic. They were marked by prayer, with people bowing to pray six to eight times per service. All throughout the services, they were praying and seeking God. People shook, shouted, spoke in tongues, and prophesied. At times, people were slain in the Spirit all over the building, as those who had fallen in battle. Some reported actually seeing glory over 312 Azusa Street.[43]

Although he didn't see it, Bartleman believed this claim. Because the presence of the Lord was so strong, he related that he had to stop blocks away from the mission on more than one occasion and pray for strength to continue to the meeting.[44]

For three years, the services were held three times a day, every morning, afternoon, and night. It has also been stated that the services generally lasted from 10:00 a.m. until 12:00 a.m. every day.[45] Bartleman described the meeting as nonstop; at any hour, day or night, people could be found there, seeking God under the power of the Holy Spirit.[46] Azusa was never empty, nor closed.

Frank Bartleman described the meetings in this manner: "Demons are being cast out, the sick healed, many blessedly saved, restored, and baptized with the Holy Spirit and power."[47] He also said, "Men's hearts are being searched as with a lighted candle" and, "Strong men lie for hours under the mighty power of God, cut down like grass. The revival will be a worldwide one, no doubt."[48]

One of the many miraculous manifestations occurring regularly was the gift of tongues, explicitly where individuals understood the language the tongue was native to. On one occasion, a missionary from the Philippines came for the purpose of disproving tongues.[49] Yet when he arrived, he heard the language from a hostile tribe close to the Philippines being spoken and knew that this occurrence was surely of the Lord. These kinds of stories are so numerous that it would be hard for one book to contain them all.

One lady went into a trance for three days after she was healed. She saw heaven and earth. Also, she received the gift of the Hebrew language. Her pastor, who was astute in Hebrew, heard her and knew she had no prior knowledge of this language. Yet he heard her quote the Twenty-Third Psalm. Bartleman's stories like this were "too numerous to take space to mention."[50]

Seymour was the pastor and leader of the Azusa Street Revival. Saying that he let the Spirit lead the services would be an understatement. He stayed humble, never taking credit for what was happening or seeking glory for himself.[51] The revival services were unlike any service in our modern era. No special sermons or speakers were announced. If people had a word, they were allowed to share. Yet if they were trying to self-promote, they'd end up sitting down embarrassed. God Himself would defend this great work. They might fall to the ground, unable to continue, and then repent. As Bartleman said, "The meeting did not depend on the human leader."[52] He also stated, "Pride and self-assertion, self-importance, and self-esteem, could not survive there. The religious ego preached its own funeral quickly."[53] He further described what would happen to those who tried to speak at Azusa when God was not speaking to them:

> The breath would be taken from them. Their minds would wander, and their brains reel. Things would turn back before their eyes. They could not go on. I never saw one get by with it in those days. They were up against God. No one cut them off; we simply prayed—the Holy Spirit did the rest. We wanted the Spirit in control, so they were carried out dead, spiritually speaking. They generally bit the dust in humility, going through the process we had all gone through.[54]

How refreshing these meetings must have been. The Almighty reined in the flesh. The Spirit guided the meetings. There was freedom for God to speak through anyone, yet if a word wasn't from God, He Himself would silence the individual.

Seymour wasn't known for his great oratory skill. He was known for his prayer life and powerful anointing when preaching. It wasn't his articulation that carried great impact;

it was an empowerment of the Holy Spirit, carried by his deep humility. In *God's Generals: Why They Succeeded and Why Some Failed*, Roberts Liardon writes that often during the services, Seymour could be found behind the two shoe crates stacked on top of each other, serving as the pulpit. He would have his head in the top one, praying.[55]

Seymour's preaching was a powerful combination of prayer and humility. John G. Lake said of Seymour's preaching,

> He had the funniest vocabulary. But I want to tell you there are doctors, lawyers, and professors, listening to the marvelous things coming from his lips. It was not what he said in words; it was what he said from his Spirit to my heart that showed me he had more of God in his life than any man I had ever met up to that time. It was God in him that attracted the people.[56]

What a contrast to many models in the West today, where the preachers' charisma and personality do the attracting. May we take a note from Seymour and let God do the drawing.

I would like us to stick our heads in old Azusa Street for a moment. Imagine the scene in this humble building. The floors are covered in sawdust, and the altars are packed with straw around them so people can kneel. Some people are sitting on the pews made of boards resting on top of old nail kegs. Others sit on makeshift chairs scattered throughout the building. Some are careful due to the low ceiling crossed with a beam to support the building. People are in the "Upper Room," seeking the baptism of the Holy Spirit. William J. Seymour has his head in the makeshift pulpit's top shoe crate, seeking God in earnest prayer. The saints are fervently praying, and the presence of God is so strong that some people are falling under the power of God before they even enter the building. Some are weeping, some are in travail, some are crying out in repentance, while some are under the power of God in a trance.

Then all of the sudden, one of the many powerful miracles takes place of a lame person being healed for all to see. Can you see Seymour coming up from the crates, lifting his humble hands, giving glory to God for the miracle, and declaring for the saints to give God glory too? The folks lift their hands and weep in the presence of God for all He is doing. Just maybe they begin to sing a chorus exalting the blood of Jesus.

This would be one scene in one service, not to mention the three services per day that continued nonstop well into the night. Salvations, healings, deliverances, and the unexplainable presence of God were the norm in old Azusa.

Never forget this: revival started with divine hunger, with fasting and prayer. Hungry people began to call on the name of the Lord to send forth a mighty outpouring. A city began to hunger for God to break in with power. Seymour, the leader and catalytic voice, continued to intensify his prayer and devotion, until he was praying seven hours a day for a year and a half before revival broke.

Before we move on to the miraculous power, glory, healings, salvations, and birth of a plethora of Pentecostal movements around the world, it would do us good to pause and reflect on how miraculous a birth this move of God really had. The Azusa Street Revival takes away any excuse anyone may have about why God wouldn't use him or her, or anyone else for that matter. Seymour was persecuted just for his skin color. He grew up in a time of explicit racism and bigotry. He didn't possess economic status. He was disabled and physically scared from smallpox, which caused him to go half blind. The Bible school he attended for a short time didn't allow him to tarry at the altar since Parham wouldn't allow Black and white people to do so together. Seymour wasn't even allowed to sit in the classroom with white people. Jim Crow laws and segregation should have made it impossible for him to lead a global revival, because it was basically unheard of for Black and white people to attend the same church together.

Also, the building Azusa used was dilapidated. They didn't have a denomination backing them. No big-name donors were underwriting the ministry or revival. There wasn't anything aesthetically to draw people. Every cultural norm during this time would have deterred people from coming, not encouraged them. They didn't have a stately building. They didn't have a paid staff. They didn't have a slick marketing campaign. But I'll tell you what they did have: They had the power of God. They had the favor of God. They had the presence of God.

As we saw, Jesus is very comfortable appearing and making Himself known in humble, simple places just like Azusa. God introduced Jesus, who was and is the King of the world, in a time when Jews were not esteemed. The cultural norms of the day placed Jews as inferior, and they were marginalized and persecuted due to their race. Like Jesus, Seymour didn't complain about his situation. Although it wasn't in an explicit teaching, Seymour seemed to embody his lowly state as a servant and take comfort that this was how Jesus had operated, according to Philippians 2:7–8, which says He "emptied himself, by taking the form of a servant, being born in the likeness of men. And being found in human form, he humbled himself by becoming obedient to the point of death, even death on a cross." Jesus showed great humility in emptying Himself and coming to earth as a ruling King not to be served, but to serve; not to demand what was owed Him, but rather to lay it down. He became a slave to serve and didn't cling to His rights. His humility took Him all the way to the cross, where He died a murderer's death. Yet He didn't defend Himself.

Here, we can see the influence of Jesus' humility on Seymour's life. Although Seymour was persecuted, he didn't demand his God-given human rights. He was marginalized, yet he understood that since Jesus had endured, he could as well. Like Jesus, he didn't play the victim card. He didn't get distracted or offended by how he was treated by Parham or others in the Church or society of his day. A humble life and start seemed to be the right order for Seymour as he reflected on his Savior and how Jesus handled Himself.

This cannot be glossed over. If Seymour had felt entitled, it would have tainted the revival. If he had been walking with an offense, it would have grieved the Spirit, and God would have more than likely chosen someone else. Seymour didn't walk around as a victim. Instead, at every setback and shortfall, when it would have been easy to give up and let someone else fight the battle, Seymour stayed low and prayed until a breakthrough. The combination of his unwavering determination, beautiful humility, and steadfast prayer allowed Jesus to use him as a catalyst for revival. So let's put aside any possible excuses. Like Seymour, let's press on to the prize. Let's turn to the fruit of persistent, steadfast prayer, laced with humility and a humble beginning, and see what God will do. There is great power in humility and faithfulness.

Revival is an act of God. Some would argue it's a sovereign move of His Spirit. Yet God has always chosen to partner with men and women in His work. In revival, there is the element of sovereignty. However, it seems always to be preceded by the great hunger and humility of a remnant of individuals who come to the place where they fully realize their utter dependence upon God and His mercy.

IGNITING PRAYER

God, give me the grace to pray like the saints of Azusa Street. Help me embody their humility and walk in their great faith. You provided grace to them and through them, and you can do the same in this generation.

Help me also walk in the Spirit in such a manner that I don't carry offense. Help me walk in forgiveness and in the unbroken fellowship with the Holy Spirit that these Azusa saints possessed.

God, send revival to my nation. Do it again, Lord! Do as you did at Azusa! In Jesus' name, Amen.

I Will Do My Part

The Power of Small Beginnings

One of the great moves of God that preceded Azusa by nearly a year was the great Welsh Revival from 1904–1905. It was a catalyst that affected some of the pioneers of Azusa, two of whom were Joseph Smale and Frank Bartleman. Wales, where it took place, was in spiritual decay.[1] Many described the Church of that day there as being secularized. Evangelistic fervor and godliness were the exceptions, not the rule. We know the Church serves as the salt of the earth, and when it loses its saltiness, society's moral and spiritual decay will soon follow. Outside the Church, the people's immorality was deplorable. One description of the Church in Wales at that time compared it to the story of Peter and his friends going fishing, and how they labored and caught nothing.[2]

What would turn the tide? How would the Church respond? Would there be a remnant of people with holy desperation? Yet despite the condition of the Church, there were individuals and families in churches throughout Wales who set their faces toward heaven in earnest prayer. Day by day, week by week, month after month they prayed, expecting God to send revival. There was a conviction amongst those who prayed in those days that revival was sure to come and that the tides would turn. The nets would be thrown, and a supernatural catch would occur.

One of these praying families was the Roberts family. They lived in a mining town called Loughor and were well respected. In their humble cottage, little did they know, they were raising up a Gideon who would take the land for God. They had seven sons, one by the name of Evan. One of the area's ministers, Rev. Arthur Goodrich, said of young Roberts, "Whatever else can be said about Evan Roberts? He was always good, always straightforward and earnest."[3]

What a great testimony. Never forget the power of godly parents raising their children in the way they should go. Parents should pray with their children and live a godly life, so their children's eyes can see it. May our children see us ever in prayer, living righteously, and witnessing often.

"Bend Me! Bend Us!"

Evan Roberts began to work in the coal mines with his father at the age of twelve. He would come home very tired, and unless he had a church meeting, he would settle in and read. His favorite book was the Bible. He would take it into the mine with him, and in any spare moment he had, he could be found reading it.

Evan would also spend hours in his room, alone with God. Prayer was dear to his heart, and he loved spending time with the Lord. His mother believed that he would frequently pray all night. She once stated that his prayer life "was more important to him than food."[4]

Evan was emphatically different from all the other young people.[5] He never took part in sports. He wasn't involved in the amusements of others his age, nor did he partake in any coarse joking. While other young men went out on dates, Evan would more than likely be found in a church service or praying. This is how God led Evan. I'm not saying a person has to determine to live as Evan did, if God hasn't spoken specifically about such a lifestyle. It's not a sin to play sports. Yet if God calls someone to lay certain things down, he or she must obey.

One night, Evan had an encounter where he received a powerful gift of discernment. Evan described this encounter in his own words:

> One night while praying by my bedside, I was taken up to a great expanse without time or space. It was communion with God. Before this, I had a far-off God. I was frightened that night, but never since. So great was my shivering that I rocked the bed, and my brother, being awakened, took hold of me, thinking I was ill. After that experience, I was awakened a little after one o'clock every night. This was most strange, for I slept like a rock through the years, and no disturbance in my room would awaken me. I was taken up into the Divine Fellowship for about four hours from that hour. I cannot tell you what it was except that it was divine. At about five o'clock, I was allowed to sleep again until about nine. About this time, I was taken up into the same experience as in the earlier morning hours, until about twelve o'clock.[6]

After this encounter, Evan went to school to prepare for the ministry. While he was there, God began to deal with him that the time was urgent and that the Holy Spirit would equip him for whatever he needed. He found himself caught up in prayer far more than in his studies.

During this time, he caught a cold and rested in bed for four days. While in bed, he was caught up in God's presence and had a vision where he saw many of his countrymen headed for hell, while the Church seemed completely paralyzed. In his vision, he walked into a garden with his Bible in hand. He looked out and far away, seeing a face filled with hatred, contempt, and scorn while laughing in a defiant manner. He then saw another figure in white robes, with a sword that was on fire. The white-robed angel began to swing the sword from side to side, and the first figure instantly disappeared. He referred to this vision in a future sermon, noting that everything he saw had come to pass, with nothing left out.

Remember, Evan wasn't in full-time ministry at this point; he was still in Holy Ghost preparation for all God had for him to do. Still hungry for more of God and impartation, he was persuaded by friends to go hear an evangelist named Seth Joshua. He had no idea that Rev. Joshua had been praying that God would raise up an "Elisha" from a common person and "mantle him with power."[7] Joshua was disturbed by a growing trend that gave more credence to intellectualism than to the Spirit, and he prayed specifically that God would raise up a young man from the coal mines.[8] Little did he know that the answer to his prayer would be sitting in the meeting that night. And he would soon hear of a young evangelist named Evan Roberts whom God would use to literally shake the entire nation of Wales and greatly impact the spiritual condition of the whole world.

While Joshua was preaching that night, there must have been some resistance upon the service.[9] He was very sensitive to the Spirit. Toward the end of the service, he began to pray, "Bend us—bend us—bend us, O Lord!"[10] Many would say that this night was the birth of the revival in Wales. Evan Roberts would go on to repeat this phrase countless times in his own meetings later. A witness of this meeting recounts that soon after the prayer of "Bend us," Evan rolled out of his seat into the aisle. He was semiconscious and lay prostrate on the floor, sweating profusely for an extended amount of time. It was described as the day he died and rose in new life.[11] During the encounter, Evan prayed, "Bend me! Bend me! Bend me! Bend us!"[12] After this encounter, Evans said, "Now a great burden came upon me for the salvation of lost souls."[13] What an encounter he had that day. His life would never be the same.

One source describes what Evan did when he returned to school after the encounter: "Day and night, without ceasing, he prayed, wept, and sighed, for a great spiritual awakening for his beloved Wales. Hours were spent in unbroken, untiring intercession, to the chagrin of those who did not understand the symptoms and secret of soul travail."[14] Back at school, in the chapel for a service one Sunday night, Evan had yet another vision of young people from his hometown compelling him to come back and teach them the ways of the Lord. He described the vision and what would follow in his own words:

> I shook my head impatiently and strove to drive away this vision, but it always came back. And I heard a voice in my inward ear as plain as anything, saying: "Go and speak to these people." And for a long time, I would not. But the pressure became greater and greater, and I could hear nothing of the sermon. Then, at last, I could resist no longer, and I said, "Well, Lord, if it is thy will, I will go." Then instantly the vision vanished, and the whole chapel became filled with a light so dazzling that I could faintly see the minister in the pulpit, and between him and me the glory as the light of the sun of Heaven.[15]

At this moment, Evan knew God was calling him to leave Bible school and head to his hometown. He left immediately for Loughor to hold a revival at the old Methodist Chapel. This was in November 1904.

Reflecting for a moment on the life of Evan Roberts, we see that he had many divine encounters. For three months, God would wake him up in the middle of the night and in the morning, for a total of seven hours a day of divine visitation. During these times, he might be taken to heaven, or have a physical visitation from the Lord, or experience God's indescribable presence, with audible instruction. He didn't go into great detail, yet we know that he had encounters that for three months were beyond comprehension. He had opened-eyed visions on at least two documented occasions, possibly more. After Joshua prayed, "Bend us," Evan recounts that the Spirit clearly told him, *This is what you need*, meaning that the flesh must be crucified.

Just Listen and Obey

These are some of the countless encounters Evan Roberts had before his ministry began. Many saints of old had powerful encounters with God before they were used mightily, including Moses, Jacob, Samuel, Gideon, Abraham, Peter, and Paul, to name a few. You might read these accounts of believers like Evan Roberts and think, *I would really like to have an encounter like that.*

Understand that Evan's encounters didn't just pop out of heaven. He consecrated himself and didn't participate in the activities of his peers. He didn't date or participate in sports. From the age of twelve, he gave himself to prayer and the study of the Word. He gave himself to the local church and attended every time a service was conducted. It's easy to say we would like what he had, but are we willing to pay the price he paid to receive impartation and encounters?

Walking in power and encountering God are not for the faint of heart. We must give ourselves to prayer, fasting, and the Word. I encourage you not just to desire encounters and spiritual impartation, but to seek the presence and face of Jesus, for however long it takes. Whether it takes six months, six years, or six decades, if you seek Him with all your heart, in His timing He will come, and you will be changed forever. It may not look like it did for Evan Roberts, but He will come. For Moses, it was a bush on fire. For Samuel, it was the audible voice of God. For Jacob, it was a live wrestling match with an angel. For Abraham, it was a divine visitation. For Peter, it was the outpouring of the Holy Spirit. For Paul, Jesus showed up in the middle of a journey. We cannot define when or how it will be for us, but we must seek God's face.

Do you want revival like Evan would soon witness? Seek Jesus, and He will give it to you. It isn't cheap. It will cost you everything. Not everyone will understand. Oh, but it will be worth it!

Ask God what adjustments you need to make. Don't copy someone else. Ask God first. He may lead you to pattern your life after someone, but let Him tell you how. Don't just try to do what Evan Roberts, William Seymour, or Charles Finney did. God may ask you to do exactly what they did, but let Him tell you that. He may say to double your prayer time, go on a fast, fast every week, read the Word an hour or more a day, go to Bible school, or pray in tongues more. Just listen and obey. As you do, you will have a fresh encounter, and if you continue, you could be the next Roberts, Seymour, or Finney.

Remember, however, that Evan Roberts didn't start out by putting in the long hours we saw evident in his spiritual life. Before his ministry would take off there was a progression, just as we observed with Steve Hill and William Seymour. Increase as God leads you from where you are today, not from where you feel you should be in ten years. Also, don't condemn yourself by comparing your prayer life to other people's. That isn't the Lord. Allow the prayer life of others to challenge you to go higher, but not to make you feel defeated and condemned.

A Cry Arises for a Nation

When Evan Roberts arrived home, he announced that Wales would soon experience the greatest revival it had ever experienced, and in fact it would be within the next two weeks.[16] He spoke to his pastor about having meetings with the young people, and his pastor obliged him. In the first meeting, only seventeen were in attendance. The next night, he ministered on the importance of the baptism in the Holy Spirit. He stressed that the only way revival would come was to co-labor with the Holy Spirit.

The night after that, he spoke on four major points that empower and move any revival forward. These points became part of many of his future messages. He asked his listeners,

> Do you desire an outpouring of the Spirit? Very well, four conditions must be observed. 1.) Is there any sin in your past that you have not confessed to God? On your knees at once. Your past must be put away, and yourself cleansed. 2.) Is there anything in your life that is doubtful? Have you forgiven everybody, everybody, EVERYBODY? If not, don't expect forgiveness for your own sins. You won't get it. 3.) Do what the Spirit prompts you to do. Obedience—prompt, implicit, unquestioning obedience to the Spirit. 4.) A public confession of Christ as your Savior. There is a vast difference between profession and confession.[17]

Evan was then asked to speak at the Sunday night service. This would be the seventh day of the meetings. That night, sixty young people gave their lives to Christ. It was at this meeting that he taught the people to pray, "Send the Spirit now for Christ's sake."[18] That service didn't end until after midnight.

The next night, the beginning of the second week, the prayer meeting was packed. The chapel was filled to capacity for the first time in its history for a prayer meeting.[19] Evan preached that the last chapter of Malachi would be fulfilled.[20] The people were awe struck by the authority and power in which he preached. Many were crying profusely, while others cried out in agony. The meeting didn't end until 3:00 a.m.

A burden for souls was falling upon the people. They were taking their eyes off personal blessing, and the cry was arising for a nation to be saved. A brokenness and holy unction to pray filled the atmosphere. This is what revival looks like— people broken over what God is broken over, people weeping over what God is weeping over. This wasn't a meeting for those simply wanting another touch from God. This was a meeting of holy desperation, crying out to a holy God to rescue a nation. When today's Church begins to pray like this, we will have revival with the same depth of God's presence and power as many experienced in yesteryear.

On Tuesday, November 8, the very next night, the atmosphere was a bit cold. Evan prayed it would break. Note that he didn't preach through it. He didn't exhort through it. He didn't have the worship team sing through it. He prayed through! The Church must take note of this. Too much of modern-day Christianity is built around preaching and singing, and very little around prayer and intercession. Evan showed us a different way. Let's let him teach us.

The meeting didn't end until the early hours of the next day. Evan and the praying saints did indeed break through. His prayer that rang throughout that meeting was that the love of Christ shown on Calvary would break through.[21] That next Wednesday morning at 6:00 a.m., the town was awakened by droves of people heading to the church to pray. It was said that "The whole town was rapidly becoming a prayer meeting."[22]

Think about this! This is not hyperbole, metaphor, or exaggeration. It wasn't merely the whole church. It wasn't half the city. It wasn't all the church leaders. Every one of those realities would have been wonderful. Yet it was the *whole town* that was turning into a prayer meeting. The coffee shop was a prayer meeting. The market was a prayer meeting. The police station was a prayer meeting. The church was a prayer meeting. God stepped in from ongoing prayer, which led to a night of prayer, which rendered a dynamic breakthrough. If God turned the city, the whole city, into a prayer meeting, God could do the same in your city, in your town! Imagine your entire city changed in a matter of weeks. We would soon see the whole nation becoming a prayer meeting.

Where are the Evan Robertses of our day? I tell you, he is no longer here, but you are! Pick up the mantle and strike the ground. Wrap it around about you. Make up your mind that you will pray until a breakthrough comes. In Jesus' name, pick up the mantle!

The next two nights, the crowds were so dense that it was unbelievable. Shops began to close so people could attend the meetings. Steel and tin workers showed up in their work clothes by the droves to get in. The Cardiff *Western Mail* newspaper reported what was taking place. One article's headline read, "Great Crowds of People Drawn to Loughor."[23] After these meetings, the news reported daily on the birth of this historic revival.

On Friday, November 11, the chapel was filled again with some eight hundred people. It was prayer, prayer, prayer! Not preaching, preaching, preaching! Those in attendance that night were gripped with a burden to pray.

On Monday, November 14, Evan preached in another chapel. It was in Aberdare, at Ebenezer Congregational Chapel.

One thousand people filled the chapel that day. From then on, he would begin to travel throughout the nation to preach and wouldn't stay in his hometown. He began to spread the fires of revival throughout the nation. The next night in Aberdare, the entire neighborhood was stirred, and people didn't go to work, but attended the prayer meeting that lasted four hours. Tremendous crowds filled the chapel, and Evan moved about, clapping his hands in holy ecstasy. He declared that the entire nation would experience revival and that Aberdare was opening the gates for it to come. By the end of the meeting the entirety of Wales, and Great Britain, for that matter, knew that revival had come to the whole of the United Kingdom.

It wasn't Evan's eloquence or communication ability that brought men to their knees—it was his tears.[24] He would fall in the pulpit from the burden and agony he would feel for the lost, while many others fell throughout the meetings under the power of God. It was common for a whole congregation of people to fall to their knees in prayer and cry out to God. It wasn't the preaching that stirred them to prayer, but God Himself through Evan's brokenness.

Revival Takes Hold of a Nation

As the Welsh Revival continued, it hit a point where more people were attending prayer meetings than had previously attended church on Sunday mornings before the revival. Churches nationwide were packed for prayer, with standing room only and people gathering outside. Churches that could hold eight hundred were now packed with fifteen hundred. Revival had taken hold of a nation.

One year into the revival, it was clear that there was no stopping it.[25] The entirety of Wales felt the impact. Hardened sinners, drunks, gamblers, and thieves were converted. The ponies the coal miners used to do the hauling were accustomed

to and understood orders filled with profanity. When the miners were saved, they cleaned up their language, so the ponies
no longer understood what they were to do and nearly halted
their work until they adjusted to the new clean language of
the workers. The courthouses were nearly empty due to the
dramatic drop in crime. Entire football and rugby teams were
gloriously saved. Young men had a burden to pray far greater
than to play. Dance clubs were empty, and bars were deserted,
with many going completely out of business. Yet the prayer
meetings were packed. Theaters closed, and prostitutes were
being saved and starting Bible studies.[26]

Just a few weeks into the revival, ten thousand conver-
sions were recorded.[27] Within only a couple of months, thirty
thousand were saved.[28] In just six months, seventy thouand
strong were now new members of the Kingdom of God. In
nine months, the total climbed to one hundred thousand new
converts. Wow! With no modern forms of communication or
marketing, around one hundred thousand people were swept
into the Kingdom. In 1904, the combined total membership for
Welsh churches stood at 48.94 percent of the nation's population, and then rose to about 56 percent by the end of 1905.[29] To
put this in perspective, if this were America it would mean that
17,500,000 people, or around 5 percent of the country's population, would get saved in nine months. This would be historic.

This revival wasn't birthed through charisma. It wasn't
birthed through elaborate lighting and stage presence. A sharp
marketing campaign didn't draw in the people. The intellectual
prowess and education of young Evan Roberts were not the
draw. It was indeed the presence and power of God, birthed
through prayer. One hundred thousand were saved because
believers sprinkled throughout Wales began to cry out for a
nation. If God did it then, He can do it again.

Remember that even though this revival wasn't based on
powerful preaching, the content that Evan preached played a

pivotal role. He didn't shrink back on sin and repentance. Repentance preaching is key to any long-standing revival, period. The Church must preach a straightforward message, including getting right with God and getting sin out. In today's westernized culture, that message can be viewed as archaic, but it is the thread of every revival that witnessed national change.

Evan Roberts is gone, but you are here. Pick up the mantle of intercession. Pick up the mantle of agony. Pick up the mantle of tears. Pick up the mantle of holy desperation. Pick up the mantle of brokenness. As you do, Evan may just be looking down from the great cloud of witnesses who are rooting for you. Right now, cry out to God and ask Him to impart to you the burden of prayer for revival!

The Hebrides Revival

What a historic move of God Wales experienced. Not far from the center of the Welsh Revival were the Hebrides Islands in Northern Scotland. The region was in desperate need of a move of God. In 1949, the presbytery of Lewis in Northern Scotland felt the burden of their desperate need for a spiritual awakening.[30] They wrote a letter to their churches and people concerning the lack of spiritual power and authority within the Church. They addressed carelessness toward church attendance and public worship. The young people had succumbed to a spirit of pleasure and possessed little, if any, regard for the things of God. The letter was a call to repentance, and to a move away from apathy. These men pleaded with their constituents to warn young people about the cinema and bars. Peggy and Christine Smith, two sisters who would be used mightily to pray for revival in Lewis (and whom I'll talk more about in a moment), recalled that not a single young man or young woman attended church before the revival.[31] Not one!

It is neither legalistic nor a laughing matter to plead with young people to avoid the worldliness the Bible warns about—drunkenness, dancing at clubs, immorality, attending certain movie theatres to watch movies filled with fornication, four-letter words, perversion, and the list goes on (see 1 Corinthians 6:9–10). Christians are sometimes entertained by many films and sitcoms that depict actions or outright sins Jesus died for. We could also add the powerful influence of some secular music with sex-charged lyrics in every genre. Many secular artists and their music videos aggrandize alcohol and drugs, along with provocative dress, sexual innuendo, and explicit perversion. Jesus died for the forgiveness of fornication, addiction, lust, and rebellion. Of all people, Christ-followers should be grieved by sin instead of being entertained by it. Something is off when sinful things entertain believers who feel no grievance from the Holy Spirit within. The West especially needs to cry out for mercy and to understand that we are not rich, but are blind, naked, and poor, with a desperate need for a heaven-sent revival that includes repentance and conviction.

There was a small group of men from Barvas, a district on the Island of Lewis, who had the same concern as the presbytery and began to seek God.[32] They were deeply burdened with the state of the Church and the island, and they began to meet in a small wooden barn to pray earnestly for revival. As they were praying, they realized that God is a covenant-keeping God. They were assured that if they kept their part of 2 Chronicles 7:14, God would indeed keep His: "If my people who are called by my name humble themselves, and pray and seek my face and turn from their wicked ways, then I will hear from heaven and will forgive their sin and heal their land."

These men would meet three times a week at around 10:00 p.m. and pray with their minister. They would wait on God until four or five o'clock in the morning. Their pastor, Rev.

James Murray MacKay, would lead them.[33] Those praying for revival in Barvas had four guiding principles made clear to them. First, they must be rightly connected to God themselves. Second, God being a covenant-keeping God, they were convinced that He would do so. Third, they concluded that they should have no preconceived ideas of how God would move. It would be His way, and not according to their outline. Fourth, there would be outward manifestations of God.[34] This would force observers to conclude that this was the working of God and not man.

Regarding the first principle of revival the Barvas men were guided by, that they must be rightly connected to God themselves, one of the deacons arose and read Psalm 24:3–5 (NIV): "Who may ascend the mountain of the LORD? Who may stand in his holy place? The one who has clean hands and a pure heart, who does not trust in an idol or swear by a false god They will receive blessing from the LORD." After he read this, he exhorted everyone to search their heart by asking, "Are our hearts clean? Is the heart pure?"[35] After the young deacon said this, he fell to his knees in a trance. Then he was on the floor. The rest fell on their knees in response and began to confess. In rededication, they began to travail in prayer more earnestly than before. Three of the men were lying prostrate, completely exhausted. However, by five o'clock in the morning, the glory of God filled the barn and would soon spread out to the entire community of Lewis.

At the exact same time, two elderly ladies ages 82 and 84, who had been praying for revival for years and who knew these Christian brothers had gathered during that time, decided to join them from their house and pray through the night as well. These sisters, Peggy and Christine Smith, were accustomed to praying all night and did so twice every week. They would get on their knees at ten o'clock at night and not get off until three or four o'clock the next morning. One of them was stone blind, and the other was bent over with arthritis. Suddenly one night, the glory of the Lord swept through their cottage. During that time God spoke to them, telling them He was going to use a mighty man of prayer by the name of Rev. Duncan Campbell. "In two weeks," said the Lord, "I shall send upon this community the greatest spiritual awakening it has known."[36]

The Smith sisters sent a request for Rev. Campbell to come in two weeks, and he responded: "It is impossible for me to come at this time but keep on praying, and I will come next year."[37]

Upon reviewing his reply, they responded, "That is what man has to say. God has said that he will be here in two weeks."[38]

Little did Campbell know it, but the sisters were right. The meeting he was scheduled to speak at elsewhere was suddenly canceled because another conference in the area at the same time had booked the majority of the hotel rooms, so there wouldn't be enough accommodations for those traveling in for the convention Campbell had been engaged for. Therefore, within two weeks he was in Barvas instead!

When Campbell arrived, he was exhausted but was asked to make an address at nine o'clock on the way to his quarters, and get supper right after. He obliged and preached. Not a lot happened during his address. There was a subtle sense of God's presence, but not much beyond that. He gave the benediction, and as he was walking down the aisle to leave, suddenly the young deacon who had prayed Psalm 24 in the barn stood and looked up to heaven and said, "God, you can't fail us. God, you can't fail us. You promised to pour water on the thirsty and floods upon the dry ground. God, you can't fail us."[39] He soon fell to his knees and went into another trance.

At that very moment, the church doors swung open—it was eleven o'clock at night—and a local blacksmith declared, "Mr.

Campbell, something wonderful has happened. Oh, we were praying that God would pour water on the thirsty and floods upon the dry ground, and listen, He's done it! He's done it!"[40]

As Campbell walked out of the church, he was astonished. There were six hundred people outside on the lawn. Where had they come from? What had made them come? One hundred of them had come from a local dance, or what we today would call a club for young people, where they were drinking and dancing the night away. During the dance, the Spirit of God fell upon them. No one made an announcement. No one gave them an invitation. No one was preaching to them.

I'll tell you exactly what happened: God heard the prayers of the people, God heard the men who had been praying in the barn for months! God heard the Smith sisters crying out for over two years! God heard that young deacon who decreed the promise of God, and He acted! It was God at center stage.

Charisma couldn't draw six hundred in, with one hundred young people suddenly leaving a party, especially as it was reported that not one youth attended church in that area. This was God at work, not marketing nor preaching ability. Nor a great personality. Nor a stately building. It was the Holy Spirit, and none other! These people weren't invited to the meeting and didn't even know of a special service. The Holy Spirit drew them in by deep conviction. What a miracle!

"Is There Mercy for Me?"

People made their way into the church by the hundreds. A building that could hold eight hundred was now packed to capacity. One of the many people getting right with God was a young lady lying prostrate on the floor, crying out to God. Moments earlier, she had been unconcerned about her soul as she danced the night away. Now, she was front and center at the pulpit, crying out to God. Here are her very words: "Oh

God, is there mercy for me? Oh God, is there mercy for me?"[41] This meeting lasted until four o'clock in the morning. No one gave an appeal. No one gave an altar call. A hallmark of the Hebrides Revival was that God did the calling. The leaders felt that this was what real revival encompassed. It was the Holy Spirit Himself who did the drawing. Here's one definition of *revival* that came out of this spiritual awakening:

> *This is revival:* When men in the streets are afraid to open mouths and utter godless words lest the judgments of God should fall; when sinners, overawed by the Presence of God tremble in the streets and cry out for mercy; when, without special meetings and sensational advertising, the Holy Ghost sweeps across cities and towns in supernatural Power and holds men in the grip of terrifying Conviction; when "every shop becomes a pulpit, every heart an altar, every home a sanctuary" and people walk softly before God . . ."[42]

Rev. Campbell didn't leave that meeting until 4:00 a.m. As he left, some encouraged him to go to the police station. He inquired as to why he was needed there, and they told him four hundred people were gathered there as conviction had fallen on the entire community. On the way there, he heard people crying out in the streets for God to have mercy on them. One detail to note is that the police station was in close proximity to the two elderly Smith sisters who were catalysts of prayer in the revival. Coincidence? I think not!

Arriving at the police station, Campbell witnessed a scene he would never forget for the rest of his life. Multitudes were crying out to God. He heard one man crying, "Oh, God, hell is too good for me! Hell is too good for me!"[43]

Now imagine the scene and what happened on the first night of this historic revival. After a season of intense prayer for years from the two sisters, and months of deep intercession from the men of Barvas in a barn, revival was now sweeping the Isle of Lewis. The young deacon intercessor prayed, and God shook the island. As I noted previously, Campbell's message wasn't very moving. It wasn't his sermon; it was an act of God. People walked out of the meeting to witness six hundred uninvited people drawn to the church in the middle of the night. One hundred left a dance party under deep conviction, not the persuasion of man, to show up at the church. Six hundred individuals in different parts of Barvas in the middle of the night woke up to the conviction and presence of God. They turned on the lights of their cottages and wandered out in the yard, feeling God Almighty upon them. He, and He alone, led them simultaneously, one by one, to the same place, all under conviction of sin. They all began to migrate to a church.

Most assuredly, many of them had never been to that par ticular church in their lives. Miles away, another four hundred went to the police station at the same exact time, crying out in repentance, "God, have mercy!" As they made their way to the police station, people were out in the street, on the sides of the roads, and some were wandering about the town, crying out to God for Him to have mercy. Wow! This was revival!

God from Start to Finish

God arrested at least a thousand people that first night of the Hebrides Revival, with no advertising or marketing. It was indeed prayer igniting revival and giving birth to a spiritual awakening. No person can take credit for this! No prepared plan would have drawn this up. No amount of education could produce this. Charisma wasn't the foundation. Pristine buildings couldn't manufacture this. This was God from start to finish! This resulted from broken people calling on Him, and God moving in a sovereign manner.

Imagine this in your town or city: Tonight, 100 percent of your city shows up at the churches, and the buildings are all packed. People clear the bars, leave the clubs, put down the alcohol, and step away from the concerts. Simultaneously, every police station is overwhelmed by people deep in confession and repentance—all at one time! No one invited them. No one marketed the moment. The only thing you can attribute it to is God answering the remnant of prayer warriors.

If God did it then, He can do it again. This was the constant flow throughout the Isle of Lewis for *three whole years*. The stories in this account I am giving you weren't the only ones, either. There are more than I have room to mention. They were normative. But I will share two more powerful, faith-building stories from this mighty outpouring. The first is about what Campbell felt was one of the most powerful moments of the revival.[44] He went to the parish of Arnol, where the city's ministers didn't understand the revival and opposed it. Their opposition affected the attendance of the locals, even while many traveled from other parishes to attend. The fruit of the meetings wasn't making much local impact. Observing the resistance, an elder told Campbell, "There is only one thing we can do. We must give ourselves to prayer—Prayer changes things."[45]

Campbell certainly agreed. A man offered his farmhouse for a prayer meeting, so Campbell and about thirty other men went there and began to pray. The going was tough, and they could feel resistance. Campbell called on a local blacksmith to pray. At this point, there was no breakthrough. It was now about one o'clock in the morning, and this man had been quiet up until this point. However, he began to pray and didn't stop for thirty minutes. He then paused and looked up to heaven and said, "God, did you know that your honor is at stake? Your honor is at stake! You promised to pour floods upon dry ground, and, God, you're not doing it!"[46]

When he prayed that prayer, the house literally shook, and a jar fell off a shelf and broke on the ground. The house began to vibrate like a leaf, and they compared it to Acts 4, when the apostles prayed and the building shook.[47] Campbell could only stand in silence as wave upon wave of divine power began flowing through the farmhouse.[48] As the house was rattling, little did its occupants know that it released a spiritual earthquake throughout all of Arnol. Simultaneously, God swept through the entire community. Campbell gave the benediction, and they began to leave the farmhouse. As they walked out, the scene was electric. Once again, people began to congregate, bringing stools and chairs, and asked, "Is there any room for us in the churches?"[49]

When Campbell left the meeting, he walked to another house to get a drink. When he walked in, he saw the entire household in tears, crying out to God for mercy. Within forty-eight hours, the local bar was closed. It never reopened. Fourteen of the regulars from this particular bar could now be found engaged in prayer three nights a week, from ten o'clock until after midnight. They would pray for the spread of revival and for their associates to get saved. Within forty-eight hours, almost every young person in Arnol between the ages of 12 and 20 surrendered to Christ. It was understood that every male from 18 to 35 could be found in a prayer meeting.

The second story I want to tell you took place in the parish of Bernera. The churches there were very cold, with little to no prayer. Campbell came there with the praying men from Barvas. Halfway through his message, the resistance was so strong that he stopped when he realized he couldn't preach his way through. This wasn't the first time he would stop a meeting in the middle of his sermon to pray. He understood the power of prayer.

Campbell called upon a young man named Donald Smith,

who stood up and cried out in deep agony of soul, reminding God that He was a "Covenant-keeping God."[50] Suddenly, the heavens were opened, and the Spirit of the Lord fell in great power not only in the church, but in the entire community of Bernera.

This was a hallmark of this great Hebrides Revival. When people prayed, God didn't just touch the church, but the whole city or community. People everywhere were suddenly gripped by the convicting power of God. People everywhere were now under an overwhelming presence of God. People who were working could work no longer because of the manifestation of the Holy Spirit's presence. Construction workers, teachers, fisherman, merchants—all undone by God. By ten o'clock, the roads in Bernera were packed with people streaming from every direction to the church. When Campbell stepped out to see the scene, a wind of the Spirit swept over the entire crowd. Many trembled in the fear of God under conviction, many wept, and some fell to the ground, burdened over their sin. Three men were found on the side of the road under such distress about their sin that they couldn't even speak.

One contributor to the local paper wrote an article referring to the movement and noted, "More are attending weekly prayer meetings than attended public worship on the Sabbath."[51] Another account notes,

> So tremendous was the supernatural moving of God for conviction of sin that not a home, not a family, nor an individual, escaped fearful conviction, and even the routine of business was stopped that the island might seek the face of God like Nineveh of Bible days. The town was changed, lives and homes transformed, and even the fishing fleet, as it sailed out into the bays, took with it a presenter to lead them in prayer and singing of hymns.[52]

What a revival! The Hebrides Revival was marked by deep repentance and the overwhelming presence of God. It was marked by weeping. It was marked by trembling. It was marked by people falling under an awful burden of sin and rising cleansed and made new.

Outstanding Components of Revival

Campbell said there were three outstanding features of this revival.[53] First was the overwhelming presence of God. For this presence to be fully understood, Campbell said it must be experienced.

The second feature was the deep conviction of sin. Campbell would often have to stop preaching so the people could repent of their sins.

Thirdly were the manifestations, mainly the prostrations and people falling under the power of God. Campbell would go on to say that attributing this work to the devil would be very close to blasphemy.

This revival was birthed by an intense season of prayer. It was birthed by a remnant of seven men from Barvas, and by the two Smith sisters, who were all desperate for a move of God. I want to submit a major takeaway from this powerful revival. What was one of the main components that kept this revival moving after it was birthed through prayer? What caused bar after bar to close in parish after parish? What caused every household in these communities to suddenly come under conviction and cry out to God with absolutely zero marketing or advertising? What caused city after city to have people confessing at the police station? What caused work to stop over and over again in parishes throughout the Hebrides? What caused the house to shake once revival started?

Note that it was not the preaching! I am an evangelist and believe in preaching, and I know we must have sound biblical preaching for the Church to be healthy. Yet in the West, we are absolutely addicted to preaching. We almost idolize good preaching. In this Hebrides Revival, as well as in the Welsh Revival, when Duncan Campbell or Evan Roberts would preach and wouldn't see a breakthrough, these men had sense enough to stop and pray. I have never seen that in the West. People simply leave. In many churches, they wouldn't even know how to pray.

Do you know how they counted converts in the Hebrides Revival? Converts weren't counted by mere confession, altar response, or church attendance. They were counted by those who attended the prayer meeting. It was later written that "Absence from the prayer meeting 'meant a doubted conversion.'"[54] What would happen if we counted converts that way in the West?

These revivals continued and thrived because these men refused to preach when they hit a wall. They stopped and called on the intercessors to pray. When they did, another breakthrough would manifest, and God would grip an entire region—not only in the meeting, but in the whole city.

I would submit that the Western Church should ask God when and where to do this. We can no longer rely on our preaching, great music, state-of-the-art buildings, programs, and personality. *We must have revival*, which means stopping the normal church train and crying out until something breaks. Until the heavens open. Until revival sweeps a city and not just a church altar.

Prayer births revival and sustains it. There is power in small beginnings, in seven men praying in a barn or two sisters praying far into the night. O God, teach us this powerful lesson. Raise up another praying band like the men of Barvas and the elder Smith sisters. May we value people's gifts to pray down revival, not solely value the gifts of singers and preachers. *Amen and Amen!*

IGNITING PRAYER

Jesus, I commit to you to do my part. I will pray for revival and awakening in my generation. I refuse to look at cold, stale religion and will lift my eyes to what you have already done. Jesus, I will set my faith and believe that what you did in the past, you will most assuredly do again.

Holy Spirit, help me continue to press in when I feel weary and tired. Give me the grace every day to seek your presence like the intercessors of the Hebrides Revival. Just as they became eyewitnesses of revival, which equated as the fruit of their intercession, I pray that I will see the fruit of my intercession in our day. I know that there is power even in a small beginning and that prayer births and sustains revival. Let it begin in me!

I Will Pick Up the Mantle of Prayer

The Power of Letting Revival Start with Me

What encouragement we should now possess after hearing the manner in which God used these generals of the faith, from those we found in the Word of God all the way to those used in modern-day times, like Charles Finney, Duncan Campbell, and Steve Hill. Here is the real fact: if God used them, He could use you.

One of the common denominators of every central figure in this book is that they are no longer with us on Earth, but are now part of the great cloud of witnesses rooting us on. I want to submit to you that their mantles are on the ground, waiting for someone to pick them up. The reason I make such a bold statement is because I look at the landscape of Christianity, and I have this question: Where are the Charles Finneys, William Seymours, Duncan Campbells, Father Nashes, the praying men of Barvas, the Smith sisters, the Steve Hills, and Leonard Ravenhills? Where are those like Maria Woodworth-Etter,

Kathryn Kuhlman, Aimee Semple McPherson, Smith Wigglesworth, John G. Lake, Reinhard Bonnke, Oral Roberts, David Wilkerson, and John Wesley? Where are the likes of powerful intercessors from biblical times such as Nehemiah, Hannah, Jacob, Moses, Daniel, and the Apostles, just to name a few?

Where are the praying men and women who married prayer and evangelism in such a magnificent way? It seems as if they have all left the building. However, it doesn't have to be this way. God is looking for someone somewhere to carry His burden, coupled with a cry toward heaven of *Pick me! Pick me!* Asking God to pick you and give you past mantles isn't arrogant or prideful. It's simply acknowledging that we need what these past generals of the faith had. We need what they had—not just to reside in history books, but to manifest in our day and time.

Thank God for the Azusa Street Revival, the Hebrides Revival, the Welsh Revival, Brownsville, and every other move of God. But these moves of God have something in common: it's what God did *then*. We need a move of God *now*. I am thankful for what God has done, but I also want to be part of what God is doing. I'm not satisfied learning about the history of awakenings; I want to be in one, especially when this world is in such desperate need of a true, heaven-sent revival.

May we no longer be satisfied with the state of the Church, nor of the nations, for that matter. God is looking for a remnant, like in Haggai's day, Hannah's day, or Seymour's day. Remember, the revivals we just observed didn't start with multitudes. The majority were similar to the Hebrides Revival, where a few dedicated intercessors prayed until something broke. You don't need an army; you need just a handful, or even just yourself. Draw a circle in the sand, stand in it, and ask God to send revival right there. May it start with you! May it start with a few that are hungry, and then may it spread to a region, a state, a nation, and eventually the entire world.

Ask God for a mantle. Maybe it's Finney's mantle you cry out for, or perhaps Smith Wigglesworth's mantle. Maybe it's the Smith sisters' mantle, or the men of Barvas's mantle, where you carry a deep burden for revival in prayer. Maybe it's someone's mantle whom I didn't mention. Just begin to ask God for the mantle of revival and awakening. Pick it up and strike the ground, in Jesus' name!

May the metrics of what a healthy church looks like be affected by the metrics of what a healthy church looked like in Acts. As I mentioned earlier, one radical form of the Hebrides Revival was that they didn't count converts by mere church attendance, but only by those who attended the prayer meeting. Many healthy church models look at attendance and budgets. But what about the manifest presence of God? What about people in the church understanding how to cast out demons? What about the entire congregation involved in winning the lost? What about the members praying for the sick outside the four walls of the church? I'm not talking about a radical remnant being engaged, but about the entire Body of Christ, which was normative in the book of Acts and should be our model. It's not about being the fastest-growing group of believers gathered, or about the top charismatic speaker on television. It should be about what the early Church possessed.

May God give each and every one of us a fresh burden for the presence of God, Gospel proclamation, healing, deliverance, and signs and wonders being part of the metric that defines a healthy church and a healthy believer. I know we're far from this reality. I know this will have to be a work of the Spirit. I also know that at the same time, we cannot be okay with continuing as we are. We must contend for change, no matter how long we need to pray. The days of settling for the status quo must go!

Why not you? Why not now? You can be an agent of change. Ask God what He would have you do. It's not a formula; it's about obedience. Seymour went from praying five hours a day to seven hours a day. That's what God told him to do. I am submitting to you to ask God how He wants you to expand your walk and devotion. I'm not calling everyone to be like Seymour. I'm saying that if your prayer life is inconsistent or has been the same for years and years, it's time to seek God and ask Him what He wants you to change. Then be obedient. If we continue to do what we've always done, we're going to continue to get what we've always gotten, and the nations are getting worse, not better.

Maybe God will tell you to be consistent every day, and that will be where you start. Maybe God will ask you to move your devotion from thirty minutes per day to an hour. What God tells you may not be what He tells someone else. Some may feel God telling them to step out and attend Bible school to prepare for full-time ministry. God may tell others to quit their job and pursue Him with everything they have. He may tell yet others to stay in their job, make it their ministry, and bring the Kingdom of God wherever they go. One of us is not greater than the other; it's about obeying and following God's leading. So do whatever He tells *you* to do. There is power in letting revival start with you.

The fact is that God is calling everyone to a higher level, and that looks different for each believer. God is calling us all to cry out for a fresh move of His Spirit. God is calling everyone to cry out for the next Great Awakening. Will you be part of the remnant who will cry out? Will you ask God to mantle you like one of the saints of yesteryear? Will you strike the ground and not settle for where you are now, or where the Church is now?

If your answer is *yes*, step in and cry out! Get around a remnant of like-minded people. Expect an increased anointing. Believe for a fresh mantle. Don't waiver or allow discouragement to set in. This is the hour! Now is the time! The next Great Awakening is on the horizon! Seize the moment!

Remember this, and never forget it: *prayer ignites revival, and it is the catalyst for every spiritual awakening.*

Acknowledgments

This work would not be possible without the support of my loving wife, Trisha. Her steadfast support never ceases to amaze me. My mother, Linda Oden, and my father, Bobby Oden, prayed me into the Kingdom, and I would never have written a book on prayer, let alone be walking with God, if it were not for their steadfast prayers. I also want to thank the late evangelist Steve Hill for planting the seeds of revival deep within me from the years I worked with him in Dallas all the way back to my time at the Brownsville Revival. If I tried to list everyone that has played a key role in my life, we would be here a long time, but I cannot leave out Dr. Bob Gladstone and Dr. Michael Brown. They not only played a pivotal role during my time at the Brownsville Revival School of Ministry but also spoke into this work. To God be the glory!

Notes

Introduction

1. James M. Gray, "O Lord, Send a Revival!," in *Living Gospel Songs & Choruses* (Chicago: Tabernacle Publishing Company, 1925), 91; see also https://hymnary.org /hymn/LGSC1925/91.

Chapter 1 I Want to See Awakening

1. "Charles Haddon Spurgeon > Quotes > Quotable Quote," Goodreads Inc., accessed September 5, 2023, https://www.goodreads.com/quotes/74181-if-sinners -be-damned-at-least-let-them-leap-to.

2. Personal interview with Jeri Hill, October 15, 2022.

3. Personal interview with Ronnie Roas, November 2, 2022.

4. Personal interview with Larry Art, October 15, 2022.

5. Interview with Jeri Hill.

6. Interview with Jeri Hill.

7. Personal interview with David Ravenhill, November 3, 2022.

8. Interview with Jeri Hill.

9. Personal interview with Mark Oberbeck, November 9, 2022. Mark was a friend of Steve's and would travel with him and serve in missions work on some of his teams. He was with Steve when Steve was touched as Sandy Miller prayed for him.

10. Personal interview with Ken Draughon, November 12, 2022.

11. Interview with Ken Draughon.

12. Personal interview with Richard Crisco, November 15, 2022.

13. *Wikipedia*, s.v. "Brownsville Revival," last modified May 26, 2023, https://en .wikipedia.org/wiki/Brownsville_Revival.

14. For the complete version of his list, see Winkie Pratney, *Revival: Principles to Change the World*, ed. Diana L. Burton (Springdale, PA.: Whittaker House, 1983), 14–15.

15. Pratney, *Revival*, 14.

16. Pratney, *Revival*, 14.
17. Pratney, *Revival*, 15.
18. Interview with Jeri Hill.
19. Interview with Jerri Hill.
20. Personal interview with John Kilpatrick, December 10, 2022.

Chapter 2 I Will Not Be Denied a Breakthrough

1. I talked to Dr. Paul Saba in August of 2023. For more information, see Paul Saba, MD, *Made to Live: A Physician's Journey to Save Life* (Winnipeg, Manitoba: Word Alive Press, 2020), or visit https://www.madetolive.com.

2. My thoughts in this paragraph and the next have been informed by Herbert Wolf, *Judges*, in *Deuteronomy, Joshua, Judges, Ruth, 1 & 2 Samuel*, vol. 3 of *The Expositor's Bible Commentary*, ed. Frank E. Gabelein (Grand Rapids: Zondervan, 1992), 376–379.

3. For more on this idea of Samson seeing, wanting, and taking whatever was right in his own eyes, see Mary J. Evans, *Judges and Ruth: An Introduction and Commentary*, vol. 7 of *Tyndale Old Testament Commentaries*, eds. David G. Firth, Tremper Longman III (Downers Grove, IL: IVP Academic, 2017), 168.

4. For more on this, see Daniel I. Block, *Judges, Ruth*, vol. 6 of *The New American Commentary: An Exegetical and Theological Exposition of Holy Scripture*, ed. David S. Dockery (Nashville: B&H Publishing Group, 1999), 426.

5. Block, *Judges, Ruth*, 425.

6. For more on this, see Block, *Judges, Ruth*, 453–454; see also Barry G. Webb, *The Book of Judges*, part of *The New International Commentary on the Old Testament*, eds. R. K. Harrison and Robert L. Hubbard Jr. (Grand Rapids: Eerdmans, 2012), 399.

7. Block, *Judges, Ruth*, 478.

8. For more on this, see again Block, *Judges, Ruth*, 478–479. In this section of text about Micah and his mother, I gleaned from the insights given on pages 478–490.

9. Block, *Judges, Ruth*, 483–484.

10. Block, *Judges, Ruth*, 485–489.

11. Block, *Judges, Ruth*, 485–489.

12. Block, *Judges, Ruth*, 490.

13. For more on this, see V. Philips Long, *1 and 2 Samuel*, vol. 8 of *Tyndale Old Testament Commentaries*, eds. David G. Firth, Tremper Longman III (Downers Grove, IL: IVP Academic, 2020), 53.

14. My thoughts in this section have been informed by Dale Ralph Davis, *Focus on the Bible–1 Samuel: Looking on the Heart*, in *Focus on the Bible Commentaries* (Scotland, United Kingdom: Christian Focus, 2010), 1 Samuel, 30, 35.

15. For more on this, see Long, *1 and 2 Samuel*, 53.

16. David Toshio Tsumura, *The First Book of Samuel*, in *The New International Commentary on the Old Testament*, eds. R. K. Harrison and Robert L. Hubbard Jr. (Grand Rapids: Eerdmans, 2007), 104.

17. Long, *1 and 2 Samuel*, 36.

18. For more on this, see Ralph W. Klein, *1 Samuel*, vol. 10 of the *Word Biblical Commentary*, 2nd ed., eds. Bruce M. Metzger, David A. Hubbard, Glenn W. Barker, et. al. (Grand Rapids: Zondervan Academic, 2014), 6–7.

19. For more on this, see Tsumura, *First Book of Samuel*, 119–120. Some of my thoughts in this paragraph and section follow the insights in this source.

Chapter 3 I Will Confess the Sins of My Nation

1. "Top 4 Frank Bartleman Quotes of All Time," Quotes.pub, accessed September 6, 2023, https://quotes.pub/frank-bartleman-quotes.

2. Some of the ideas I talk about in this section on Jeremiah calling the nation to repentance come from J. Daniel Hay, *The Message of the Prophets* (Grand Rapids: Zondervan, 2010), 148–167.

3. For more on this horrific outcome, see Richard A. Taylor, *Haggai, Malachi: An Exegetical and Theological Exposition of Holy Scripture*. vol. 21 of *The New American Commentary* (Nashville: Broadman & Holman, 2004), 30.

4. Andreas J. Köstenberger, *A Theology of John's Gospel and Letters: The Word, the Christ, the Son of God*, in the *Biblical Theology of the New Testament* (Grand Rapids: Zondervan, 2009), 63.

5. For more on this, see Jill Middlemas, *The Templeless Age: An Introduction to the History, Literature, and Theology of the "Exile"* (Louisville: Westminster John Knox, 2007).

6. See also Köstenberger, *Theology of John's Gospel*, 63, 71, where I found some of the insights in this section.

7. Köstenberger, *Theology of John's Gospel*, 63, 71.

8. For more on this thought and the insights in some of the paragraphs that directly follow, see Taylor, *Haggai*, 30–33, 101–138.

9. For more on this thought, see Ralph L. Smith, *Micah-Malachi*, in the *Word Biblical Commentary* (Grand Rapids: Thomas Nelson, 1984), 154–55.

10. This thought, as well as some that follow in the next few paragraphs, were gleaned from Taylor, *Haggai*, 139–143.

11. Taylor, *Haggai*, 139–143.

12. Andrew E. Hill, *Haggai, Zechariah, Malachi: An Introduction and Commentary*, vol. 28 of *Tyndale Old Testament Commentaries*, eds. David G. Firth, Tremper Longman III (Downers Grove, IL: IVP Academic 2012), 72.

13. Hill, *Haggai, Zechariah, Malachi*, 72.

14. Heather Clark, "Study Reveals Most American Pastors Silent on Current Issues Despite Biblical Beliefs," Christian News Network, August 12, 2014, https://christiannews.net/2014/08/12/study-reveals-most-american-pastors-silent-on-current-issues-despite-biblical-beliefs/.

15. Dr. Michael Brown, "Why Don't More Pastors Speak Out?," ASKDrBrown *Consider This* video series, streamed live on November 7, 2018, YouTube video, 3:22–3:55, https://www.youtube.com/watch?v=gOPB2hbrqsM.

16. Brown, "Why Don't More Pastors Speak Out?," 0:56–1:20.

17. Rev. R. Casey Shobe, "Sins of Omission," Episcopal Church of the Transfiguration, November 14, 2020, http://www.transfiguration.net/sins-of-omission/.

18. Brown, "Why Don't More Pastors Speak Out?," 4:38–5:06.

19. For more on this, see Tremper Longman III and David E. Garland, *Jeremiah–Ezekiel*, vol. 7 of *The Expositor's Bible Commentary* (Grand Rapids: Zondervan Academic, 2010), 183.

20. J. Daniel Hays, *The Message of the Prophets: A Survey of the Prophetic and Apocalyptic Books of the Old Testament* (Grand Rapids: Zondervan, 2010), 157.

21. Longman and Garland, *Jeremiah–Ezekiel*, 223.

22. Longman and Garland, *Jeremiah–Ezekiel*, 223.

Chapter 4 I Will No Longer Watch Passively from the Sidelines

1. Personal interview with John Kilpatrick, December 10, 2022.

2. For more on this, see the Fire Bible: New Living Translation (Springfield, MO: Life Publishers International, 2021), 1382.

3. Hannah K. Harrington, *The Books of Ezra and Nehemiah,* in *The New International Commentary on the Old Testament* (Grand Rapids: Eerdmans, 2022), 279.

4. Derek Kidner, *Ezra and Nehemiah: An Introduction and Commentary*, vol. 12 of *Tyndale Old Testament Commentaries*, eds. David G. Firth, Tremper Longman III (Downers Grove, IL: IVP Academic, 2009), 58–59.

5. Kidner, *Ezra and Nehemiah*, 58–59.

6. Gary V. Smith, *Ezra–Nehemiah*, in the *Exegetical Commentary on the Old Testament*, ed. Daniel I. Block (Grand Rapids, Zondervan Academic, 2022), 256.

7. Smith, *Ezra–Nehemiah*, 257.

8. H. G. M. Williamson, *Ezra–Nehemiah*, in the *Word Biblical Commentary* (Grand Rapids: Zondervan, 1985), 172.

9. Williamson, *Ezra–Nehemiah*, 172.

10. Kidner, *Ezra and Nehemiah*, 85. Some of my thoughts in the next few paragraphs are based on Kidner's insights there, as well as on pages 258–259 of Smith's *Ezra–Nehemiah* in the *Exegetical Commentary*, which I cited in note 6.

11. Harrington, *Books of Ezra and Nehemiah*, 281.

12. For more on this paragraph's concepts, see Kidner, *Ezra and Nehemiah*, 86.

13. Mervin Breneman, *Ezra, Nehemiah, Esther: An Exegetical and Theological Exposition of Holy Scripture*, vol. 10 of *The New American Commentary* (Nashville: Broadman & Holman, 1993), 172.

14. Harrington, *Books of Ezra and Nehemiah*, 281. See pages 281–282 for more on this concept and the concepts I present in the next few paragraphs.

15. Note that in this paragraph and the three that follow, I have again drawn from the concepts that Kidner presented in *Ezra and Nehemiah*, 86–87, and also that Smith presented in *Ezra–Nehemiah*, 274–275.

16. For more on this, see Williamson, *Ezra–Nehemiah*, 179.

17. For more on the information presented in the rest of this paragraph, see Harrington, *Books of Ezra and Nehemiah*, 287.

18. Smith, *Ezra–Nehemiah*, 275.

19. Harrington, *Books of Ezra and Nehemiah*, 284.

20. This idea comes from Breneman, *Ezra, Nehemiah, Esther*, 176.

21. Smith, *Ezra–Nehemiah*, 276. Again, note that Smith's work in this commentary has informed some of the thoughts I express here on this topic.

22. Harrington, *Books of Ezra and Nehemiah*, 291–292.

23. For further thoughts on this paragraph's concepts, see Williamson, *Ezra–Nehemiah*, 191.

24. Smith, *Ezra–Nehemiah*, 279.

25. National Center for Health Statistics, "Unmarried Childbearing," Centers for Disease Control and Prevention (CDC) online, last reviewed January 31, 2023, https://www.cdc.gov/nchs/fastats/unmarried-childbearing.htm.

26. "Parenting in America: 1. The American family today," Pew Research Center, December 17, 2015, https://www.pewresearch.org/social-trends/2015/12/17/1-the-american-family-today/.

27. OECD Family Database, "SF2.4: Share of births outside of marriage," Organisation for Economic Co-operation and Development, updated December 2022, https://www.oecd.org/els/family/SF_2_4_Share_births_outside_marriage.pdf.

28. Wilkinson and Finkbeiner, "Divorce Statistics: Over 115 Studies, Facts and Rates for 2022," accessed April 2, 2023, https://www.wf-lawyers.com/divorce-statistics-and-facts/.

29. Wilkinson and Finkbeiner, "Divorce Statistics."

30. Wilkinson and Finkbeiner, "Divorce Statistics."

31. "Marriage and Cohabitation in the U.S.," Pew Research Center, November 6, 2019, https://www.pewresearch.org/social-trends/2019/11/06/marriage-and-cohabitation-in-the-u-s/,

32. "Marriage and Cohabitation," Pew Research Center.

33. "Key findings on marriage and cohabitation in the U.S.," Pew Research Center, November 6, 2019, https://www.pewresearch.org/fact-tank/2019/11/06/key-findings-on-marriage-and-cohabitation-in-the-u-s/.

34. "About six-in-ten Americans say legalization of same-sex marriage is good for society," Pew Research Center, November 15, 2022, https://www.pewresearch.org/fact-tank/2022/11/15/about-six-in-ten-americans-say-legalization-of-same-sex-marriage-is-good-for-society/.

35. Justin McCarthy, "Record-High 70% in U.S. Support Same-Sex Marriage," Gallup.com, June 8, 2021, https://news.gallup.com/poll/350486/record-high-support-same-sex-marriage.aspx.

36. Remy Tumin, "Same-Sex Couple Households in U.S. Surpass One Million," the *New York Times* online, https://www.nytimes.com/2022/12/02/us/same-sex-households-census.html.

37. Jeffrey M. Jones, "One in 10 LGBT Americans Married to Same-Sex Spouse," Gallip.com, February 24, 2021, https://news.gallup.com/poll/329975/one-lgbt-americans-married-sex-spouse.aspx.

38. "June 2022: By the Numbers," United States Census Bureau, accessed March 27, 2023, https://www.census.gov/library/spotlights/by-the-numbers/june/.

39. "LGBT Populations," MAP (Movement Advancement Project), last updated June 28, 2023, https://www.lgbtmap.org/equality-maps/lgbt_populations.

40. Julie Moreau, "Adult children of lesbian parents less likely to identify as straight, study finds," nbcnews.com, April 2, 2019, https://www.nbcnews.com/feature/nbc-out/adult-children-lesbian-parents-less-likely-identify-straight-study-finds-n989976.

41. "Gender Dysphoria Diagnosis," American Psychiatric Association, accessed September 9, 2023, https://www.psychiatry.org/psychiatrists/diversity/education/transgender-and-gender-nonconforming-patients/gender-dysphoria-diagnosis#:~:text=In%201990%2C%20the%20World%20Health,an%20effort%20to%20reduce%20stigma.

42. Robin Respaut and Chad Terhune, "Putting numbers on the rise in children seeking gender care," October 6, 2022, https://www.reuters.com/investigates/special-report/usa-transyouth-data/.

43. Respaut and Terhune, "Children seeking gender care."

44. Respaut and Terhune, "Children seeking gender care."

Chapter 5 I Will Not Be Moved by Dire Circumstances

1. I gleaned some of the thoughts in this paragraph from Beth Kreitzer, ed., *New Testament: Luke*, vol. 3 of *Reformation Commentary on Scripture*, gen. eds. Timothy George and Scott M. Manetsch (Downers Grove, IL: IVP Academic, 2015), 346–348.

2. Arthur A. Just Jr., *Luke*, vol. 3 of *Ancient Christian Commentary on Scripture* (Downers Grove, IL: IVP Academic, 2003), 276.

3. Joel B. Green, *The Gospel of Luke*, part of *The New International Commentary on the New Testament* (Grand Rapids: Eerdmans, 1997), 639. In fact, a number of the thoughts in this paragraph are gleaned from page 639 of this resource.

4. For more on the thoughts in this sentence and the next, see Karen H. Jobes, *1, 2, & 3 John*, vol. 19 of *Zondervan Exegetical Commentary on the New Testament*, ed. Clinton E. Arnold (Grand Rapids: Zondervan, 2014), 708.

5. These further insights into the widow and her tenuous position were also informed by Green, *The Gospel of Luke*, 640.

6. For more on this, see Jobes, *1, 2, & 3 John*, 709.

7. These contrasts are taken from Richard B. Vinson, "The God of Luke–Acts," in *Interpretation: A Journal of Bible and Theology* 68, no. 4 (2014), 563–564.

8. Vinson, "God of Luke–Acts," 564.

9. This interesting comparison of the widow to a boxer comes from Green, *Gospel of Luke*, 641.

10. Vinson, "God of Luke–Acts," 564.

11. Robert H. Stein, *Mark*, part of the *Baker Exegetical Commentary on the New Testament* (Grand Rapids: Baker Academic, 2008), 519.

12. William Lane, *The Gospel of Mark*, part of *The New International Commentary on the New Testament* (Grand Rapids: Eerdmans, 1974), 409.

13. Lane, *Gospel of Mark*, 410.

14. Stein, *Mark*, 520. See also page 519 for more on this.

15. Mark L. Strauss, *Mark*, vol. 2 of *Zondervan Exegetical Commentary on the New Testament*, ed. Clinton E. Arnold (Grand Rapids: Zondervan, 2014), 499.

16. Lane, *Gospel of Mark*, 410.

17. The thoughts in this paragraph are based on Lane, *Gospel of Mark*, 411.

18. I. Howard Marshall, *The Epistles of John*, part of *The New International Commentary on the New Testament* (Grand Rapids: Eerdmans, 1978), 244.

19. Marshall, *Epistles of John*, 245. Some of this section of text includes further thoughts gleaned from Marshall about praying according to God's will.

20. In addition to Marshall's work, for more on this see Robert W. Yarbrough, *1–3 John*, part of the *Baker Exegetical Commentary on the New Testament* (Grand Rapids: Baker Academic, 2008), 300.

21. Yarbrough, *1–3 John*, 300. See also pages 301–302 for more on this.

22. Marshall, *Epistles of John*, 245.

23. J. I. Packer, *Praying the Lord's Prayer* (Wheaton, IL: Crossway Books, 2007), 51–53.

24. Packer, *Praying the Lord's Prayer*, 53.

25. Packer, *Praying the Lord's Prayer*, 59.

26. The ideas in this paragraph and the next are gleaned from Karen H. Jobes, *1, 2, & 3 John*, vol. 19 of *Zondervan Exegetical Commentary on the New Testament*, ed. Clinton E. Arnold (Grand Rapids: Zondervan, 2014), 231–232.

27. Yarbrough, *1–3 John*, 302.

28. Marshall, *Epistles of John*, 245.

29. For more on the ensuing discussion about the words of James, see Craig L. Blomberg and Mariam J. Kamell, *James*, vol. 16 of *Zondervan Exegetical Commentary on the New Testament*, ed. Clinton E. Arnold (Grand Rapids: Zondervan, 2008), 52–53.

30. For more on this, see Dan G. McCartney, *James*, part of the *Baker Exegetical Commentary on the New Testament*, eds. Robert W. Yarbrough and Robert H. Stein (Grand Rapids: Baker Academic, 2009), 91. In fact, this paragraph and the next two are informed by McCartney's work.

31. McCartney, *James*, 91.

32. McCartney, *James*, 91.

33. This paragraph is drawn from Scot McKnight's work in *The Letter of James*, part of *The New International Commentary on the New Testament* (Grand Rapids: Eerdmans, 2011), 92.

34. See again Blomberg and Kamell, *James*, especially page 54, which informed my thoughts for the rest of this section.

35. Blomberg and Kamell, *James*, 54.

36. Blomberg and Kamell, *James*, 54.

Chapter 6 I Will Cooperate with the Holy Spirit

1. See also Andreas Köstenberger, *A Theology of John's Gospel Letters* (Grand Rapids: Zondervan, 2009), 437–439.

2. For more on this, see Eckhard J. Schnabel, *Acts*, vol. 5 of *Zondervan Exegetical Commentary on the New Testament*, ed. Clinton E. Arnold (Grand Rapids: Zondervan, 2012), 84.

3. For more on this concept, see I. Howard Marshall, *Acts: An Introduction and Commentary*, vol. 5 of *Tyndale New Testament Commentaries* (Grand Rapids: IVP Academic, 2008), 67.

4. John B. Polhill, *Acts*, vol. 26 of *The New American Commentary: An Exegetical and Theological Exposition of Holy Scripture* (Nashville: Broadman & Holman, 1992), 90.

5. For more on this, see Darrell L. Bock, *Acts*, part of the *Baker Exegetical Commentary on the New Testament*, eds. Robert W. Yarbrough and Robert H. Stein (Grand Rapids: Baker Academic, 2007), 104.

6. See also Schnabel, *Acts*, 120.

7. Bock, *Acts*, 151. In the rest of this paragraph, I parallel Bock's insights on this topic.

8. Craig S. Keener, *Acts: An Exegetical Commentary* (Grand Rapids: Baker Academic, 2013), 2:1044.

9. Keener, *Acts*, 2:1047.

10. For more on this, see Schnabel, *Acts*, 210.

11. F. F. Bruce, *The Book of Acts*, part of *The New International Commentary on the New Testament* (Grand Rapids: Eerdmans, 1988), 98–99.

12. For more on this paragraph's concepts, see Schnabel, *Acts*, 239, and Bruce, *Book of Acts*, 92–93.

13. Schnabel, *Acts*, 259.

14. Schnabel, *Acts*, 259–260.

15. Schnabel, *Acts*, 329; see also page 331.

16. Schnabel, *Acts*, 336; see also page 337 for more on this.

17. Schnabel, *Acts*, 337.

18. Tony Merida, *Christ Centered Exposition: Exalting Jesus in Acts*, eds. David Platt, Daniel L. Akin, and Tony Merida (Nashville: B&H Publishing, 2017), 134.

19. Schnabel, *Acts*, 261–262.

20. Schnabel, *Acts*, 262.

21. Rosa Prince, "Work, rest and pray: American daily habits revealed," *The Telegraph* online, June 2, 2014, https://www.telegraph.co.uk/news/worldnews/north america/usa/10918301/Work-rest-and-pray-American-daily-habits-revealed.html.

22. "Religious Landscape Study: Frequency of Prayer," Pew Research Center, accessed September 12, 2023, https://www.pewresearch.org/religion/religious-land scape-study/frequency-of-prayer/.

23. "Statistics in the Ministry: Newly Revised Statistics," Pastoral Care Inc., accessed September 12, 2023, https://www.pastoralcareinc.com/statistics/.

Chapter 7 I Will Possess a Heart for the Lost

1. For more information on the Second Great Awakening, see Winkie Pratney, *Revival: Principles to Change the World* (Springdale, PA.: Whitaker House, 1983), especially 111–112.

2. Roberts Liardon, *God's Generals: The Revivalists* (New Kingston, PA.: Whitaker House, 2008), 284. Much of my information on Finney in this chapter was resourced from this book, especially pages 284–332.

3. Liardon, *Revivalists*, 284.

4. Basil Miller, *Charles Finney: He Prayed Down Revivals* (Grand Rapids: Zondervan, 1951), 10. Some of my information on Finney comes from this resource.

5. Miller, *Prayed Down Revivals*, 13.

6. Charles G. Finney, *Autobiography of Charles G. Finney: A Lifetime of Evangelical Preaching to Christians Across America, Revealed* (Coppell, TX: Pantianos Classics, 1908), 9. Some of the information in the surrounding text was gleaned from this autobiography.

7. Finney, *Autobiography*, 9.

8. Finney, *Autobiography*, 11.

9. Liardon, *Revivalists*, 291.

10. Liardon, *Revivalists*, 292.

11. Liardon, *Revivalists*, 293.

12. Liardon, *Revivalists*, 293.

13. Liardon, *Revivalists*, 293.

14. Liardon, *Revivalists*, 293.

15. Liardon, *Revivalists*, 295.

16. Finney, *Autobiography*, 30.

17. Liardon, *Revivalists*, 298.

18. Liardon, *Revivalists*, 298.

19. Daniel Kolenda told me this story once himself, but I've also heard him tell it while he was preaching.

20. Charles G. Finney, *Power from on High: What It Is and How to Obtain It* (Fort Washington, PA: Christian Literature Crusade, 2005), 52, 56.

21. Finney, *Power from on High*, 55.

22. This is from a sermon I once heard Reinhard Bonnke preach.

23. Reinhard Bonnke sermon.

24. This paragraph is based on Finney's comments in his *Autobiography* I cited in note 6; see especially page 25.

25. Charles Finney, *The Spirit Filled Life* (New Kingston, PA: Whitaker House, 2000), 117–118.

26. Finney, *Autobiography*, 25.

27. Liardon, *Revivalists*, 304.

28. Finney, *Autobiography*, 57. The rest of this section is also based on pages 57–58 of this resource.

29. Finney, *Autobiography*, 57.

30. This paragraph's historical information and the next are based on Finney's *Autobiography*, especially page 33.

31. Charles G. Finney, *The Autobiography of Charles G. Finney: The Life Story of America's Greatest Evangelist—In His Own Words* (Minneapolis: Bethany House, 1977), 49. Notice that this is a different autobiography than the one I previously cited. There is more than one Finney autobiography in print.

32. Liardon, *Revivalists*, 306. The rest of this paragraph's historical information is based on this book, particularly pages 306–307.

33. Charles Finney, *Memoirs of Charles Finney* (New York: A. S. Barnes and Company, 1876), 122–123.

34. Finney, *Memoirs*, 122–123.

35. The next few paragraphs are based on Liardon, *Revivalists*, 312.

36. Liardon, *Revivalists*, 320; see also page 312.

37. Finney, *Memoirs*, 363.

38. For more on Lydia, and on Finney's subsequent marriages, see Liardon, *Revivalists*, 330–332.

39. Catherine M. Rokicky, "Ohio History Journal: Lydia Finney and Evangelical Womanhood," Ohio History Connection, accessed April 3, 2023, https://resources.ohio history.org/ohj/browse/displaypages.php?display%5B%5D=0103&display%5B%5D =170&display%5B%5D=189.

40. This paragraph's thoughts from Finney are taken from his book *Prevailing Prayer* (Grand Rapids: Kregel, 1965), 8–9.

41. Finney, *Prevailing Prayer*, 8–9.

42. Charles G. Finney, *Lectures on Revivals of Religion* (Cambridge, MA: Belknap Press of Harvard University Press, 1960), 39.

Chapter 8 I Will Not Focus on My Limitations

1. This powerful insight is drawn from John I. Durham, *Exodus*, vol. 3 of the *Word Biblical Commentary*, 2nd ed. (Grand Rapids: Zondervan Academic, 2015), 49.

2. Some of this background information was taken from Cecil M. Robeck Jr., *The Azusa Street Mission and Revival: The Birth of the Global Pentecostal Movement* (Nashville: Thomas Nelson, 2006), 17, 19, 24.

3. Additional information and the statistics in this section were taken from Larry Martin, *The Life and Ministry of William J. Seymour and a History of the Azusa Street Revival* (Duncan, OK: Christian Life Books , 2014), 7, 31–36.

4. Martin, *William J. Seymour*, 35.

5. David K. Fremon, *The Jim Crow Laws and Racism in American History* (New York: Enslow, 2000), as cited at *Wikipedia*, s.v. "Jim Crow laws," last modified August 28, 2023, https://en.wikipedia.org/wiki/Jim_Crow_laws.

6. Malinda Maynor Lowery, *Lumbee Indians in the Jim Crow South: Race, Identity, and the Making of a Nation* (Chapel Hill, NC: University of North Carolina Press, 2010), also as cited at *Wikipedia*, s.v. "Jim Crow laws," last modified August 28, 2023, https://en.wikipedia.org/wiki/Jim_Crow_laws.

7. The historical information in this paragraph comes from Roberts Liardon, *God's Generals: Why They Succeeded and Why Some Failed* (Tulsa, OK: Albury, 1996), 140.

8. Martin, *William J. Seymour*, 39.

9. Jim Crow Museum, "Jim Crow Era," Ferris State University, https://www.ferris.edu/HTMLS/news/jimcrow/timeline/jimcrow.htm.

10. Jim Crow Museum, "Jim Crow Era."

11. Some of the information in this paragraph comes from Jerrold M. Packard, *American Nightmare: The History of Jim Crow* (New York: St. Martin's Press, 2002).

12. Unless otherwise noted, the rest of the background historical information on Seymour in this chapter is taken either from Martin, *William J. Seymour*, 70, 74, 90–95, 119, 122–131, 139–160, or Robeck, *Azusa Street*, 26–27, 45–47, 58, 67–68.

13. Grant Wacker, "Marching to Zion: The Story of John Alexander Dowie's 20th Century Utopian City-Zion, Illinois," *Assemblies of God Heritage*, Fall 1986, 8.

14. Martin, *William J. Seymour*, 95.

15. Frank Bartleman, *My Story: The Latter Rain* (Jawbone Digital, 2012), 26.

16. Bartleman, *Latter Rain*, 26.

17. Herbert L. Sutton, *Our Heritage and Our Hope: The History of First Baptist Church of Los Angeles, California, 1874–1974* (Los Angeles: First Baptist Church, 1974), 24.

18. Martin, *William J. Seymour*, 123.

19. Martin, *William J. Seymour*, 123.

20. Frank Bartleman, *Azusa Street* (New Kensington, PA: Whitaker House, 1982), 15.

21. Bartleman, *Azusa Street*, 15.

22. Note that some secondary sources incorrectly list Julia's last name as Hutchinson.

23. Kenneth Copeland, *John G. Lake: His Life, His Sermons, His Boldness of Faith* (Fort Worth, TX: Kenneth Copeland Publications, 1995), 88.

24. Martin, *William J. Seymour*, 147.

25. Martin, *William J. Seymour*, 148.

26. Martin, *William J. Seymour*, 148; see also "The Same Old Way," *The Apostolic Faith* (Los Angeles), September 1906, 3.

27. For more on Emma Cotton, see Robeck, *Azusa Street*. (You can view an online pdf version of this work at https://library.mibckerala.org/lms_frame/eBook/The %20Azusa%20Street%20Mission%20and%20Re%20-%20Cecil%20M.%20Robeck %20Jr.pdf.)

28. Liardon, *Why They Succeeded*, 147; see also Cotton, *Personal Reminiscences*, 3.

29. Martin, *William J. Seymour*, 148.

30. Martin, *William J. Seymour*, 148.

31. Martin, *William J. Seymour*, 148; also see in Douglas J. Nelson, "For Such a Time as This: the Story of Bishop William J. Seymour and the Azusa Street Revival: A Search for Pentecostal/Charismatic Roots," PhD dissertation (England: University of Birmingham, 1981), 58.

32. Russell Chandler, "Pentecostals: Old Faith, New Impact," *Los Angeles Times*, January 11, 1976, I-22; see also in Martin, *William J. Seymour*, 148.

33. Martin, *William J. Seymour*, 148; see also in John G. Lake, *Adventures in God* (Tulsa, OK: Harrison House, 1981), 3.

34. Martin, *William J. Seymour*, 159; see also in Clara Lum, "Miss Clara Lum Writes Wonders," *The Missionary World*, August 1906, 2.

35. William Seymour, *When the Fire Fell: Firsthand accounts of the Azusa Street Revival*, ed. John Campbell (Independently published, 2020), 76. The rest of this paragraph's information is from this same resource.

36. Harvey Cox, *Fire from Heaven: The Rise of Pentecostal Spirituality and the Reshaping of Religion in the Twenty-First Century* (Cambridge, MA: Da Capo Press, 2001), 262. See also Dean Merrill, *50 Pentecostal and Charismatic Leaders Every Christian Should Know* (Minneapolis: Chosen, 2021), 40.

37. For more on this section's thoughts, see David E. Garland, *Luke*, vol. 3 of *Zondervan Exegetical Commentary on the New Testament*, ed. Clinton E. Arnold (Grand Rapids: Zondervan, 2011), 120, 177–178.

38. Garland, *Luke*, 120.

39. Larry E. Martin, ed., *The True Believers: Eye Witness Accounts of the Revival That Shook the World* (Pensacola, Fla.: Christian Life Books, 1998), 178. In fact, the next several lines contain insights from this work; see pages 40–42, 178–80.

40. Martin, *True Believers*, 178.

41. Martin, *True Believers*, 40.

42. Martin, *True Believers*, 42.

43. Bartleman, *Azusa Street*, 58.

44. Bartleman, *Azusa Street*, 58.

45. Seymour, *When the Fire Fell*, 76.

46. Bartleman, *Azusa Street*, 56.

47. Bartleman, *Azusa Street*, 64.

48. Bartleman, *Azusa Street*, 64.

49. Martin, *William J. Seymour*, 182. In fact, this paragraph and the next draw their information from this source.

50. Martin, *William J. Seymour*, 182; see also Frank Bartleman, "Letter from Los Angeles," *Triumphs of Faith*, December 1906, 248–250.

51. Some of this paragraph's insights come from Ron McIntosh, *The Quest for Revival: Experiencing Great Revival of the Past, Empowering You for God's Move Today* (Tulsa, OK: Harrison House, 2023), 32.

52. Bartleman, *Azusa Street*, 56.

53. Bartleman, *Azusa Street*, 56.

54. Bartleman, *Azusa Street*, 59.

55. Liardon, *Why They Succeeded*, 154.

56. Lake, *Adventures in God*, 18–19.

Chapter 9 I Will Do My Part

1. Much of the Welsh Revival background I give in the first few pages of this chapter is gleaned from W. Percy Hicks, *The Life Story of Evan Roberts: and Stirring Experiences in the Welsh Revival* (Pensacola, FL: Christian Life Books, 2015), 19–27.

2. Hicks, *Life Story of Evan Roberts*, 20.

3. Hicks, *Life Story of Evan Roberts*, 21.

4. Hicks, *Life Story of Evan Roberts*, 24.

5. This paragraph's information was gleaned from Roberts Liardon, *God's Generals: Why They Succeeded and Why Some Failed* (Tulsa, OK: Albury, 1996), 80–81.

6. Hicks, *Life Story of Evan Roberts*, 25–26. In fact, the next story about Evan being caught up in God's presence and seeing a vision is based on pages 25–27 of this resource.

7. Liardon, *Why They Succeeded*, 83.

8. For more on this, see Colin Whittaker, *Great Revivals: When God Moves in Power* (Eastbourne, England: Kingsway Communications, 2005), 101.

9. This paragraph's information comes from David Mathews, *I Saw the Welsh Revival* (Pensacola, FL: Christian Life Books, 2016), 22.

10. Matthews, *I Saw the Welsh Revival*, 22.

11. Matthews, *I Saw the Welsh Revival*, 22.

12. Whittaker, *Great Revivals*, 101.

13. Whittaker, *Great Revivals*, 102.

14. Whittaker, *Great Revivals*, 23.

15. Hicks, *Life Story of Evan Roberts*, 31. The next two paragraphs also draw from Hicks, pages 30–31.

16. The historical background in the next few paragraphs is drawn from Whittaker, *Great Revivals*, 103–104.

17. Whittaker, *Great Revivals*, 103–104.

18. Whittaker, *Great Revivals*, 104.

19. The historical background in the next few paragraphs is drawn from John Hayward, "Timeline of the First Two Weeks of the 1904–5 Welsh Revival," version 1.0, June 2004, https://www.churchmodel.org.uk/Timeline2W04.pdf. Some of it is also drawn from Whittaker, *Great Revivals*, 104.

20. Some of this section's historical background is likewise drawn from Whittaker, *Great Revivals*, 104.

21. Whittaker, *Great Revivals*, 104.

22. Whittaker, *Great Revivals*, 104. In fact, the next several paragraphs are drawn from pages 104–106 of Whittaker's book just cited.

23. Whittaker, *Great Revivals*, 105.

24. I gleaned the information in this paragraph from Liardon, *Why They Succeeded*, 87.

25. This paragraph is based on Whittaker, *Great Revivals*, 107–108.

26. Liardon, *Why They Succeeded*, 86.

27. S. B. Shaw, *The Great Revival in Wales* (Duncan, OK: Christian Life Books, 2015), 18.

28. For more on this and on the next few statistics about the total number of people saved (100,000 of them!), visit Revival Library, "The Welsh Revival 1904," accessed September 13, 2023, https://www.revival-library.org/revival_histories/evangelical/1900/welsh_revival_1904.shtml.

29. Church Growth Modelling, "1904–5 Welsh Revival and Limited Enthusiasm," accessed September 13, 2023, https://churchmodel.org.uk/church-growth-models/limited-enthusiasm/limited-enthusiasm conversion-model/1904-5-welsh-revival and-limited-enthusiasm/.

30. This paragraph's historical information comes from Duncan Campbell's books *Revival in the Hebrides* (Great Britain: Kraus House, 2016), 1, and from *The Lewis Awakening: The Nature of a God Sent Revival* (Edinburgh, Scotland: The Faith Mission, 1954, with rights given to CrossReach Publications, 2017), 6.

31. Campbell, *Revival in the Hebrides*, 32.

32. For more on this, see Owen Murphy, *When God Stepped Down From Heaven: Revival in the Hebrides* (Independently published, 2017), 15–16.

33. For more on the birth of this revival, see also Campbell, *The Lewis Awakening*, 5–10, 32–48.

34. For more on these four guiding principles, see Campbell, *The Lewis Awakening*, specifically pages 5–10.

35. Murphy, *When God Stepped Down*, 16. See also 17–18.

36. Murphy, *When God Steped Down*, 17.

37. Murphy, *When God Steped Down*, 17.

38. Murphy, *When God Steped Down*, 17.

39. Campbell, *The Lewis Awakening*, 36.

40. Campbell, *The Lewis Awakening*, 37.

41. Campbell, *The Lewis Awakening*, 37.

42. Murphy, *When God Stepped Down*, back cover text.

43. Campbell, *Revival in the Hebrides*, 40.

44. Campbell, *Revival in the Hebrides*, 46.

45. Campbell, *Revival in the Hebrides*, 46.

46. Campbell, *Revival in the Hebrides*, 46.

47. Much of my story of these accounts is drawn from Murphy, *When God Stepped Down*, 23–25.

48. This particular image of Campbell comes from Campbell, *The Lewis Awakening*, 15.

49. Campbell, *Revival in the Hebrides*, 48.

50. Murphy, *When God Stepped Down*, 24.

51. Campbell, *The Lewis Awakening*, 23–24.
52. Murphy, *When God Stepped Down*, 23–25.
53. Campbell's comments in this section have been paraphrased from his book *The Lewis Awakening*, particularly on page 26.
54. Murphy, *When God Stepped Down*, 31.

Joe Oden burns for revival and awakening. He is a product of revival himself. He was saved and delivered from drugs during the Brownsville Revival, and he has never been the same. Joe has spent the last twenty-five years traveling throughout America and the world, equipping and mobilizing the body of Christ to share the Gospel and reach the lost. His heart burns with the desire to see people transformed by the power and presence of Jesus. He currently serves as the national prayer and evangelism director for the Assemblies of God; director of the Assemblies of God World Prayer Center; and as the evangelism commission chairman for PCCNA (Pentecostal/Charismatic Churches of North America). In addition, Joe authors several books and serves on different councils and boards, including ACPE (Association for Clinical Pastoral Education) and the executive committee for the Global Evangelist Alliance, a division of Empowered 21. Joe earned his doctorate degree from the Assemblies of God Theological Seminary.